to lead

A *Practical Guide* for Leaders in
Churches & Faith-Based Organizations

Joel Milgate

Copyright © 2023 by Joel David Milgate

Published by AVAIL

All rights reserved. No portion of this book may be reproduced, stored in a retrieval system, or transmitted in any form or by any means—electronic, mechanical, photocopy, recording, scanning, or other—except for brief quotations in critical reviews or articles, without prior written permission of the author.

Scripture quotations marked ESV are from The ESV® Bible (The Holy Bible, English Standard Version®), copyright © 2001 by Crossway, a publishing ministry of Good News Publishers. Used by permission. All rights reserved. | Scripture quotations marked MSG are taken from THE MESSAGE, copyright © 1993, 1994, 1995, 1996, 2000, 2001, 2002 by Eugene H. Peterson. Used by permission of NavPress. All rights reserved. Represented by Tyndale House Publishers, Inc. | Scripture quotations marked NASB are taken from the (NASB®) New American Standard Bible®, Copyright © 1960, 1971, 1977, 1995, 2020 by The Lockman Foundation. Used by permission. All rights reserved. www.lockman.org | Scripture quotations marked NIV are taken from the Holy Bible, New International Version®, NIV®. Copyright © 1973, 1978, 1984, 2011 by Biblica, Inc.™ Used by permission of Zondervan. All rights reserved worldwide. www.zondervan.com. The "NIV" and "New International Version" are trademarks registered in the United States Patent and Trademark Office by Biblica, Inc.™ | Scripture quotations marked NKJV are taken from the New King James Version®. Copyright © 1982 by Thomas Nelson. Used by permission. All rights reserved. | Scripture quotations marked NLT are taken from the Holy Bible, New Living Translation, copyright © 1996, 2004, 2015 by Tyndale House Foundation. Used by permission of Tyndale House Publishers, Inc., Carol Stream, Illinois 60188. All rights reserved.

For foreign and subsidiary rights, contact the author.

Cover design by: Harper Creative
Cover photo by: Luke Edwards

ISBN: 978-1-960678-54-6   1 2 3 4 5 6 7 8 9 10

Printed in the United States of America

To lead is to voyage.

This book is dedicated to all the voyagers of Curate who choose the adventure of the sea over the predictability of land.

Thank you for being a church of grace, soul, adventure, and love.

Lord, lead us into the great unknown.

contents

foreword... ix

acknowledgments... xi

author's note.. xiii

introduction: **am i doing this right?**......................15

part I. leading yourself

chapter 1. **to lead is good** 21

chapter 2. **to lead is to be an example** 39

chapter 3. **to lead is to pray**................................53

chapter 4. **to lead is to grow in the word** 67

chapter 5. **to lead is to trust** 83

chapter 6. **to lead is to learn** 97

part II. leading others

chapter 7. **to lead is to own it** 109

chapter 8. **to lead is to care** 123

chapter 9. **to lead is to serve** 135

chapter 10. **to lead is to recruit**............................145

chapter 11. **to lead is to develop**...........................157

chapter 12. **to lead is to build relationships**.................171

chapter 13. **to lead is to have vision**........................179

chapter 14. **to lead is to shape culture**.....................191

conclusion. **embark on the voyage**.........................205

    appendix 1. **spiritual practices**..........................213

    appendix 2. **theology resources**.........................215

    appendix 3. **meeting template**...........................217

    appendix 4. **debrief template**............................219

about the author..221

foreword

I met Pastor Joel Milgate a number of years ago in gorgeous Tauranga, New Zealand. We were at a gathering of pastors called Nexus, led by my good friend Pastor Paul de Jong. Everything about the day was superb: the setting, the food, the atmosphere, the vision, and the people. Yes, the people!

I met a lot of great pastors and leaders that day; however, when I met Pastor Joel, there was *that* something special about him. Have you ever met someone and felt *that* about them but couldn't put your finger on what *that* was? Some of *that* is unpacked in this book, *To Lead: A Practical Guide for Leaders in Churches and Faith-Based Organizations*.

Since our initial meeting, I've had the honor of serving Pastor Joel as a speaker and consultant to his church. He once arranged for me to have dinner with one of his leaders. This leader picked me up from my hotel and took me to his home to have dinner with his family. It was during that dinner that he and his wife shared nuances of Pastor Joel's leadership—not just in the church but in the community at large. *To Lead* reflects in writing what others who have observed Pastor Joel say about him.

This book is not a series of theoretical essays; it is a collection of chapters from the life and leadership of Pastor Joel Milgate. In this book, you will be challenged to accept your sovereign placement in life to lead where you're planted. And not just lead but to take responsibility for that space in which you're placed: in your job, in business, at home, in the community, and, yes, in the church.

To Lead is about paying close attention to your personal and professional life, knowing that He has equipped and prepared you to lead. You were born to influence others while growing and maturing yourself. You were placed on this planet with a purpose that has eternal consequences.

He is calling you to lead.

Will you?

SAM CHAND
Leadership Architect, Consultant, Strategist
Author and Speaker

acknowledgments

I want to thank my wife, Katie, for encouraging me to finally put a book out there and my kids Alessandro, Micah, Charlie, and Violet for letting me often escape to put pen to paper. Thank you to the people of Curate Church for having the grace to let me learn many of the lessons contained in these pages. To all the leaders who have come and gone over the years, thank you. And Celina, my immensely encouraging editor, thank you for helping bring these ideas to life in a way people might actually be able to read them.

author's note

Thanks for taking the time to read this book. I know there is a lot of stuff out there about leadership. But let's be honest: if you're anything like me, it can be a bit overwhelming and confusing. With so much content available at our fingertips, we can be left wondering what leading actually looks like in the daily lives of volunteer leaders in churches and faith-based organizations.

We can look at other leaders and wonder if we could ever measure up or if we have what it takes to even try. We feel like we are cut from a different cloth. We are not sure if the advice being passed on by others only works for people like them—and not anyone else. The truth is that leaders come in all different shapes and sizes, scopes and personalities, and it's my joy to distill some basics of what it looks like to lead—right where you are—in a way that's authentic to you.

What moved me to write this book was knowing that the average leader in our churches or faith-based organizations doesn't necessarily have the time or desire to pore through shelves of leadership material. This simple guide for everyday leaders is my humble attempt to fill that gap.

This book isn't so much for the senior pastor or the CEO (although I'm sure it will still help). It's for the leaders on the front lines and the coal face. The small group leader. The team leader. The middle manager. The leader, volunteering their time, effort, and, in many cases, their own finances in order to play their part in the body of Christ—while also working in other paid jobs, studying, or raising a family. The chapters are intentionally short, each concluding with a "Put This Into Practice" section.

I didn't grow up in a Christian home; however, from the moment I started walking with Jesus, I found myself being pushed into leadership opportunities. From my late teenage years until present day, I have been on a leadership journey. I don't aspire to lead as much as I desire to make a difference. It started with opportunities to lead in youth ministry and camps which led me to become a lead pastor at the age of twenty-five. I've led in church, faith-based organizations, and different companies. Being a lead pastor is where I still am today, together with my wife, Katie, leading a multilocation church in beautiful New Zealand. I love it! I feel like I have always been thrown into the deep end, and that's okay—there's something about the responsibility of the deep end that God uses to grow us.

When embarking on the voyage of leadership many years ago, I could never have imagined the places and spaces it would take me. I wouldn't have been able to comprehend either the challenges and heartaches or the joys and triumphs. Leading has kept me hungry as a follower to learn from others further ahead—one hand forward—and has kept me thinking about the others I can serve and help—one hand back. I'd love the same for you.

So, let's do it. Let's lead.

introduction:

am i doing this right?

Have you ever asked this question?
Katie and I decided to lead our first small group together in the early years of our leadership journey. We were young, had a young family, and our house was a bit of an embarrassment, but we decided to do it anyway. We invited a few people we knew and a few people we didn't know whom we had recently met at church. We felt out of our depth as this diverse group of people started turning up at our house. We had gone through the flurry of getting our kids to bed early and making our living room semi-presentable, bringing in chairs from all over our house to ensure there was enough seating. The kettle was boiled, and snacks were on the table.

As the evening progressed, I kept wondering if we were doing this right. Are we hosting right? Are we leading prayer correctly? Is the discussion helpful? Will the people who don't know others feel at ease, like they belong? How can I get this person to talk less and this other person to at least say something? I didn't know if Katie and I were doing it right or not, but we kept doing it anyway. Over the next few years, that group continued. People came and went, we became friends, we went through highs and lows, and most importantly, we encouraged each other in our discipleship journeys.

Leading on the front lines within churches and faith-based organizations is of utmost importance. It's our small groups and teams within ministries that are on the ground where leadership is really experienced, both by the leader and the people they are leading!

> **We live in a leadership paradox: in a time that needs leadership more than ever, people seem to be more reluctant than ever to take on the responsibility of leadership.**

We live in a leadership paradox: in a time that needs leadership more than ever, people seem to be more reluctant than ever to take on the responsibility of leadership. That's understandable when trust for leaders is at an all-time low due to abuse of power and the lack of integrity that have become public. However, that just means that strong leaders are more important now than ever.

There's an incredible difference that can be made if a small group leader can grow beyond fostering conversations or facilitating Bible studies—if they can become someone who leads in an environment where people genuinely do life together, engage in the spiritual practice of community, and provide pastoral care and support. If they can become a trustworthy presence, shepherding a discerning group of people who are working out the Jesus life in every part of their lives, then that's truly impactful.

The same is true for a faith-based organization team leader at any level. If they can become more than just a presence that gets things done, they can be someone who truly helps people on their team to become like Christ. They can foster love, joy, peace, integrity, faithfulness, and steadfastness. If they don't just focus on getting the job done, they can build a team through which God can work in miraculous ways.

In Romans 12:8, the word for leadership is a noun, *prostémi* (the one who goes before). In 1 Corinthians 12:28, the word for leadership is a function, *kybernesis* (administration). In Philippians 1:1, the word for leadership is a term for a person with minor responsibility, *episkopoi* (overseer; see also Acts 20:28 and 1 Timothy 3:1). In 1 Timothy 3:8, leadership represents a position of lower status, *diakonos* (servant). In Titus 1:5, the word is a descriptive term, *presbyteroi* (elders, wiser people). In Ephesians 4:11, the word is a metaphor, not a title, *poimenes* (pastors or shepherds).[1]

All of that is to say: leadership can come in many shapes and sizes.

---

1 R. Paul Stevens, *The Other Six Days: Vocation, Work, and Ministry in Biblical Perspective* (Grand Rapids, MI: William B Eerdmans Publishing Co, 2000).

Are you doing this right? Well, that's not the question you should be asking. The question is: am I willing to lead in a way that places people above tasks, God's principles above society's practices, and discipleship above numbers? Am I willing to become an example that others can follow—although imperfect—but one that is continually growing in Christ?

That's what this book is about: learning to truly lead on the front lines. You are needed, you can do it, and you can grow in it. If you say yes to this journey and continue in it, by God's grace, you will make an eternal difference in the lives of others.

> **You are needed, you can do it, and you can grow in it.**

PART I
leading yourself

chapter 1
to lead is good

"Leadership is the process of influencing others to understand and agree about what needs to be done, how it needs to be done, by influencing and facilitating others to do it."
—Gary Yukl[2]

Everything that you think is good about your life is the result of leadership. Think about that for a moment.

Everything that's good about the world is because of God's intentional leadership in creating it so. Everything that's good about civilization is because of women and men who have made it so. And everything that's good about your life is the result of the leadership of God, your parents, and others or even your own leadership in your life. Good is brought into our world through leadership. Therefore, to lead is good!

---
[2] Gary Yukl, *Leadership in Organizations* (Boston, MA: Pearson, 2006).

We can think of concrete examples like New Zealand activist Kate Sheppard, the country's most famous suffragist and the first to win the right to vote for women. She led, along with others, and through leading, accomplished good. Or perhaps Martin Luther King, Jr. and others leading the Civil Rights Movement and winning the right for African Americans to be treated equally under the law. We could think of Henry Williams and his contemporaries, working with both Māori chiefs and the Crown to ensure indigenous rights could be protected and a partnership achieved. And while we are still working towards a world in which all of humankind can experience equality and fairness, we can recognize the huge advances made so far.

We have gotten this far through leadership, and we will only be able to continue advancing through leadership. To lead is good.

To lead is good.

We can think about our own lives. I know that I wouldn't be where I am today if it weren't for those who have led me at some stage of my life. None of them led me perfectly (that's not possible, as you know!), but you don't need perfection to accomplish a lot of good. My parents led me and prepared me for life. A youth pastor studied the Bible with me. My cousin challenged me, and it was that challenge that the Holy Spirit used to lead me to Jesus. Older guys in the church spent time with me and built me up in the things of God. My pastor gave me opportunities and correction. He passed on his wisdom and allowed me to learn from failure. My small group leaders created an environment in which I could experience community and personal growth. When I became a pastor, other pastors took time to help, guide, and encourage me on my journey.

Indeed, I wouldn't be where I am if it weren't for many people leading me in all sorts of ways—some big, some small. Some may not have even realized they were leading, but they were! They accomplished good in my life.

How about you? Can you connect the good in your life to the impact of other people's leadership?

Defining Leadership

A working definition of leadership that I personally like is this one: to lead is to take responsibility for a desired future and influence others to help create it.

> **To lead is to take responsibility for a desired future and influence others to help create it.**

The second law of thermodynamics is about entropy; in our broken world, things get worse without outside or intentional stimuli. That's why we need leadership.
- We need to lead ourselves.
- We need to have leaders in our lives.
- We need to discover we were all called to lead in some way.

When people like you step up to lead, it accomplishes a lot of good. When you lead a group, a team, a new Christian, or someone struggling through a season of life, you are bringing about the good.

It was John Maxwell who wrote that "everything rises and falls on leadership."[3] And it was Craig Groeschel who wrote that "when the leader gets better, everyone gets better."[4] In a world that loves to avoid responsibility, whose tidal drift seems to be in the vortex of individualism and consumerism, we must remember that to lead is to contribute to the good. In fact, to lead as a follower of Jesus is to contribute to the good that God is doing.

If it's so good, why don't we all aspire to and engage in leadership? There are multiple reasons why people don't lead. Here are some of the most common reasons that I often hear, and I'll spend the rest of this chapter unpacking them:

- "I don't see myself as a leader."
- "I can't find a model of leadership that resonates with my personality."
- "I don't have anything to offer."
- "My culture doesn't celebrate leadership."

Sound familiar?

No matter what reason you give yourself, I want to encourage you that you are a leader. If you find yourself struggling to discover the type of leader you are meant to be, remember this: what or whom you worship is what or whom you become like. Let me explain. We can see that God the Father is a leader, Jesus the Son is a leader, and the Holy Spirit is a leader. Each part of the

---

3   John C. Maxwell, *The 21 Indispensable Qualities of a Leader* (Nashville: Thomas Nelson, 2007).
4   Craig Groeschel, Twitter post, January 26, 2018, 7:03 pm, https://twitter.com/craiggroeschel/status/957041223075815424?lang=en.

Godhead takes responsibility for a desired future and influences the heavenly realm and the Earth by their grace and mercy. God does this, so we might join in and become coworkers to see His vision come to pass.

I'm a firm believer that anyone can be a leader. In fact, I would take it a step further by stating that I believe we are all *called* to lead. As followers of Jesus, leading embodies the very nature that God is developing in us.

Demystifying Discipleship

To become a disciple of Jesus is to become someone commissioned to go and make other disciples. Jesus called Peter. He said, "Follow Me, and I will have you become fishers of people" (Mark 1:17, NASB).

We theologically understand that the Great Commission is not just a commission for the original disciples but a timeless commission to all disciples. That means you and me. That means the people we find ourselves leading right now. Jesus said:

> "Therefore, go and make disciples of all the nations, baptizing them in the name of the Father and the Son and the Holy Spirit. Teach these new disciples to obey all the commands I have given you. And be sure of this: I am with you always, even to the end of the age."
> —Matthew 28:19-20 (NLT)

Go into your world, your workplace, your small group, your community, or your classroom and make disciples. Making disciples sure sounds like leadership to me! It is seeing a desired future in someone else's life and influencing them to help create it. Now, either God is unreasonable and calling us all to do something that we can't do or—yes, you've got it—everyone can lead.

Making disciples sure sounds like leadership to me!

I'm not saying that everyone has the gift of leadership—that everyone is called to run a church or an organization. There is no doubt that God gives a grace for leadership. This grace or gift gives people different scopes of leadership, according to the specific callings they have received from God. Some are able to lead ten people, others fifty, some one hundred, and others a thousand and beyond. We see this example in relation to Moses and Israel in Exodus 18:21. We know that some people are gifted, graced, and favored leaders; however, that doesn't mean we are not all called to lead at some level. At a basic level, leading one or a few is within reach of every one of us. Don't sell yourself short of what God is calling you to do.

God Is Looking for a Leader Just Like You

We are all capable of leading. If this weren't true, we shouldn't have the basic biology that enables us to be parents—because becoming a parent is becoming a leader. As a parent, you have a little person entrusted to your leadership. You take responsibility for a desired future for them, and you influence others—mainly them—but also their teachers, friends, and wider family to help create it.

Now, I know that many people haven't had great parents present in their life. For some people, the relationship that was supposed to be the safest and most nurturing became the most terrifying and abusive. I'm deeply sorry if that has been your story. Sadly, hurt people hurt people. I'm so thankful we serve a God who heals us, uses even our deepest pain for good, and promises to redeem all things one day. If we put aside the authority figures and caregivers who really failed in their mandate for a moment and think of those who were present, loving, faithful, and safe, we can begin to see that good "parents" and, therefore, good leadership, can come in many different shapes and sizes.

My mum is highly structured, organized, disciplined, and risk-averse. But she has loved me and raised me out of who she is. My dad, on the other hand, was adventurous, highly adaptable, and generous and raised me out of who he was. Some parents are easy going and others are rigid; some extroverts, others introverts; some are outgoing, and others are more reserved. Yet with enough wholeness, love, and a bit of wisdom, all of these personalities are capable of great parenting if they choose.

The same is true when it comes to being an effective leader.

This is great news because it doesn't mean you need to be an A-type personality, an extrovert, have a certain Myers Briggs type, or have a certain Enneagram number to lead. These tools are very helpful, but they are just that—tools to aid our self-awareness and personal growth. In the same way great parents come in all shapes and sizes, so do great leaders. We need the tortoises and the hares, the loud and the quiet, the introverts and the extroverts.

All of Us Can Lead

We can lead out of who we are—out of who God made us to be. We can be an "us" type of leader. God is not looking for me to be like anyone else; God's looking for me to be a "Joel" type of leader. Yes, He wants me to have the character of Jesus but through the personality, strengths, and weaknesses of Joel. You can insert your own name here: He's looking for a _____ type of leader!

I'm convinced two of the major reasons people don't step up to become the leaders they could be is because they don't see themselves as leaders, or they don't see models of leadership like their own. I can identify so much with this in my leadership journey. I have often looked at other pastors and thought, *I can't do that.* I don't think like them, see the world like them, have their experience or have it all together like they seem to.

I have discovered that my secret weapon in leadership is being comfortable with how God made *me*.

> **I have discovered that my secret weapon in leadership is being comfortable with how God made me.**

When I read Scripture, I am encouraged by the fact that Jesus chose twelve apostles. They were all different: some were risk-takers, some were doubters, some aspired to the top positions, and others seemed pretty quiet. Some managed the money (poorly), and others collected the leftovers in baskets. Most ran away at the crucifixion. Here's the thing: God still used them all.

In the movie *You, Me and Dupree*, Owen Wilson plays the role of Randy—a man out of luck and living with his newly wed friends.[5] By the end of the movie, he finds his mojo as a motivational speaker, and it's his motivational concept in which I think we can find comedic encouragement.

Randy says we all have a "ness." It's our name plus "ness." It's what makes us unique, and when we learn to see it as a strength and release it, a power is unfurled: our Joel-ness or our Katie-ness or your Name-ness. You have a "ness."

You Have Everything You Need to Lead

Now, before you react to this, allow me to elaborate: through and in Christ, you have everything you need to lead. In fact, you have more than enough:

> By his divine power, God has given us everything we need for living a godly life. We have received all of this by coming to know him, the one who called us to himself by means of his marvelous glory and excellence. —2 Peter 1:3 (NLT)

I'm convinced that the only qualification for effective leadership is a willingness to say YES. If you have a yes towards God, you can trust Him in faith that He can use you to lead in some way, shape, or form.

I have often been plagued by insecurity and a lack of confidence. It's the enemy's classic strategy to try to keep us down and

---
5 Anthony Russo and Joe Russo, *You, Me and Dupree* (July 14, 2006; Universal City: Universal Pictures).

keep us silent. He doesn't want us to lead and make a difference for good. Too often, I have partnered with him—aligning my thoughts to his lies rather than to God's Word. God didn't tell Joshua to be strong and courageous because Joshua was awesome and had what it took. God told Joshua to be strong and courageous because God was with him (Joshua 1:9).

You don't need to have all the answers; you don't need to be at a certain magical level of maturity. You have to realize that in your flesh, you will never feel ready, but by God's Spirit, He can use you right now. You just have to be willing. The woman Jesus spoke to at the well in John 4 wasn't qualified. Her life was a moral mess, she wasn't respected in her community, and she didn't seem to have many friends. However, she had an encounter with Jesus, and it changed her. Even more significantly, she wanted that for *others*.

The day she was transformed was the same day she was commissioned to lead.

She ran back to town and told everyone to come and see. She led a great revival that day in her village. No qualifications, no degrees, no pedigree—just a sincere and willing heart. A yes. You might feel like you can't lead that group, that team, or that project. You would be in good company! Almost every leader in Scripture felt that way. (This personally makes me exhale in relief). Moses, Gideon, Jeremiah—they didn't think they were the right people. But they all discovered the same thing: with one small yes, God could use them anyway.

The right person is the willing person. And when you have God by your side—and on your inside—you have everything you need to lead.

A Word on Culture

My current cultural reference point is New Zealand. In this context, I find that there's another major reason people don't lead. I'm sure you will understand whether you live in New Zealand or not. It's our tall poppy syndrome. We don't have a culture that celebrates leadership. We cut down our leaders. We cut down the tall poppies. Those that raise themselves up find themselves cut or pulled down. We look at emerging leaders and think, *Who are you to be stepping up?* Unfortunately, it doubles down on our feelings of inadequacy.

We have to become aware of and realize the culture we are living in. It may give us an extra barrier to overcome. However, our culture is not king! Paul writes in Romans 12:2, "Do not be conformed to your culture, but instead be transformed" (paraphrased). The Message version of this verse is, "Don't become so well-adjusted to your culture that you fit into it without even thinking."

We need to understand, celebrate, and be aligned with the kingdom culture of Jesus. Heaven loves leadership. Heaven commissions leaders, celebrates leaders, and longs for every follower of Jesus to step up and lead. A kingdom culture honors leaders and values those aspiring to lead.

We must be more loyal to the culture we will live in for eternity than the temporal culture of the world around us.

> **We must be more loyal to the culture we will live in for eternity than the temporal culture of the world around us.**

A fish doesn't know what water is; it simply swims in it. A fish doesn't question the water in which it lives. The major cultural forces of our time can make us that way too if we don't awaken to them. There are cultural themes in every age that stand as opposites to the type of culture God wants to form in us. In our time, specifically in the Western world, some of these would be:

- Individualism
- Consumerism
- Materialism
- Rights over responsibilities

Individualism says it's the individual that is of paramount importance, especially when compared with the group. The individual should be free to act, to become, and to do what they will, even if it's to the wider group's or community's detriment. My personal freedom matters most. This is in direct opposition to leadership. There is a cost to leadership when it confronts a culture of individualism. Leadership requires sacrifice and calls us to be less concerned with only ourselves and more concerned with others.

Consumerism is a culture of more: the acquisition of more stuff or experiences in ever-increasing amounts, but always with ever-diminishing satisfaction. Leadership is about the opposite. Leadership calls us to contribute—to put in more than we take out.

Materialism is consumerism's close friend; it's about the obsession with things and the material world. It accumulates stuff, stuff, and more stuff and always has self at its center. A life devoted to godly leadership will often call us to give away or sacrifice the material for the eternal. Leadership cannot flourish if materialism has our heart.

We live in a time and society that are loud about the *rights of an individual* but very quiet about personal *responsibility*. I'm all about the development of human rights, especially to protect the most vulnerable and to motivate people towards helpful action. I do wonder, however, why we haven't also developed a universal list of human responsibilities. What do we expect from every human? God gave Israel (His chosen people) both rights and responsibilities through the law. Many people feel that the world should serve them, and I admittedly wonder in amusement what great things they have supposedly done to feel the world owes them so much.

The Queen of England passed away during the writing of this book. Queen Elizabeth II served her people for seventy years and 214 days. She often spoke about her sense of duty. She said, "Our modern world places such heavy demands on our time and attention that the need to remember our responsibilities to others is greater than ever."[6] Leadership is a holy responsibility.

These dominant cultural themes of our time give us much to overcome if we are going to step up to lead. Our culture is very much anti-leadership and often looks to sabotage those who do step up and lead. When we live in its waters without questioning it, we become a part of the problem.

A Transient and Distracted Culture

We are seeing fewer people—especially young people—willing to step up and lead throughout the Western context. The number

---

6 Queen Elizabeth II, "Christmas Broadcast 2002," *Royal*, 16 Nov. 2015, www.royal.uk/christmas-broadcast-2002.

one barrier to church planting and ministry growth is often a lack of people feeling called to the work or willing to shoulder the responsibility and call. I wonder how much the distractions of our modern life—social media, gaming, smartphones, and on-demand entertainment—are numbing us and slowing our maturity.

As people chase a life that they see online, I wonder if people are more transient, trying to find themselves by constantly changing context, vocation, and churches, hoping something will click into place. Now, being young and being able to explore the world and life is a gift, but there's something incredibly immature, selfish, and unhelpful to the kingdom—and destructive to our churches—when we are not settling into adulthood and displaying selflessness until much later in our lives.

To step into leadership effectively will mean committing to a place and people for a period of time. It will mean putting down roots to be challenged and pushing through the times when we want to hit the metaphorical stop button and change what we are watching.

There Is a Different Way

Jesus is a radical example of leadership. Why radical? Because He modeled a different way to lead: servant leadership.

> Have this mind among yourselves, which is yours in Christ Jesus, who, though he was in the form of God, did not count equality with God a thing to be grasped, but emptied himself, by taking the form of a servant, being born in the likeness of men. And being found in human form, he humbled himself by becoming obedient to the point of death, even death on a cross. Therefore God has highly exalted him and bestowed

> on him the name that is above every name, so that at the name of Jesus every knee should bow, in heaven and on earth and under the earth, and every tongue confess that Jesus Christ is Lord, to the glory of God the Father. —Philippians 2:5-11 (ESV)

It says He gave up *everything* and took the form of a servant; He was obedient even to death.

The path Jesus cuts leads in the opposite direction of the culture of His time—and human nature itself:

- Servant leadership is the antithesis of individualism as it puts my preferences aside to help others.
- Servant leadership is the antithesis of consumerism as it gives to others, rather than taking away from them.
- Servant leadership is the antithesis of materialism as it brings about a good beyond the collection of things and the material world.
- Servant leadership is the antithesis of rights-based culture as it calls us to lay aside our rights for the sake of Jesus and others.

> Then Jesus said to his disciples, "If any of you wants to be my follower, you must give up your own way, take up your cross, and follow me. If you try to hang on to your life, you will lose it. But if you give up your life for my sake, you will save it. And what do you benefit if you gain the whole world but lose your own soul? Is anything worth more than your soul?" —Matthew 16:24-26 (NLT)

Our time needs people who will walk the path Jesus has marked out for us. People whose lives won't be dominated by self but instead will sacrifice for the sake of others. People who won't see their church or organization as fundamentally there to serve them but will see that they can serve others in it. People who will give up the odd weekend away and prioritize living well with the people of God over their own recreation. People who understand that because they have been called into relationship with Jesus, they have been called to lead.

When we step up to lead, we are saying no to individualism, materialism, consumerism, and an overemphasis on our own rights. We are saying yes to the path of Jesus and the responsibility He is calling us to take. However, that doesn't mean it comes naturally or easily. We must overcome our own sense of inadequacy and our cultural pull to inaction and discover what leading looks like to us. But slaying these dragons of our time is totally worth it because the treasure of good awaits beyond the battle.

> **We must overcome our own sense of inadequacy and our cultural pull to inaction and discover what leading looks like to us.**

To Lead is Good.

Put This Into Practice

1. Make a list of the people who led you during different stages of your life thus far and how their leadership accomplished good in your life from which you are benefitting today.
2. Write down three things that make you unique. In other words, how would you describe your "ness"?
3. Pray this prayer each day as you become more of the leader you were always designed to be:

Heavenly Father, I'm grateful for your leadership.
Thank you for calling me to be a leader too.
I choose to believe your Word over my thoughts and feelings.
I will not partner with a spirit of fear and timidity; instead, I receive and trust your spirit of love, power, and a sound mind.
Don't let me fit so well into my culture that
I don't even feel the tension.
Transform the way I think, so I will know your ways.
I'm available to be used by you.
I trust that you in me is enough.
Give me favor with both you and people.
In Jesus's name, Amen.

chapter 2

to lead is to be an example

"We should have Christian leaders who are characterized by the relational qualities that we want everyone else to copy."
—Scot McKnight[7]

Have you ever heard the expression, "Do what I say, not what I do"?

I heard it from my dad and others a few times while growing up. It expresses the tension that all of us face in leadership between what is ideal and how we ourselves act. As a parent, I am confronted with this often. For example, I find myself frustrated and yelling at my kids because they are yelling at each other. Oh, the irony.

---

[7] Scot McKnight, *Pastor Paul: Nurturing a Culture of Christoformity in the Church (Theological Explorations for the Church Catholic* (Grand Rapids, MI: Brazos Press, 2019).

The hard truth is that the people we lead won't do what we say; they will do what we do. Our example matters most. Paul knew this when it came to leadership. That's why he wrote the following instruction to Timothy in order to guide him: "Let no one despise you for your youth, but set the believers an example in speech, in conduct, in love, in faith, in purity" (1 Timothy 4:12, ESV).

Here's some context: Timothy was sent to oversee the church in Ephesus. The church was large and prominent. Timothy was young and had been asked to lead a lot. We can deduce this had probably been stressful for him, and that's why Paul recommended he drink some wine—not to zone out or destress but to perhaps help with a stomach ulcer.

The letter from Paul, Timothy's mentor, was Paul's guidance to Timothy in the midst of this leadership challenge. And we should note that the letter is relatively void of much of what would fill such a letter if it were written these days. There's no strategic leadership advice, no quick-fix principles on how to grow the church, no new techniques to try out. Instead, the letter is a big encouragement to Timothy regarding who he is and how he is to conduct himself as a leader. Identity and integrity. Being an example. Out of that should flow what he does—reading the Scriptures, teaching, and preaching.

> **Here's where we get to the crux of leadership: being a great leader is more about presence than technique.**

Here's where we get to the crux of leadership: being a great leader is more about presence than technique.

We Create Around Us What Exists Within Us

Edwin Friedman coined the term "non-anxious presence" in his book, *A Failure of Nerve*.[8] He writes at length about the importance of the leader's presence above all else when it comes to determining leadership effectiveness. We live in a world obsessed with technique, looking for the secret sauce, the get-rich-quick scheme, or the shortcut to their destination. When it comes to godly leadership, there is no such thing. The most important thing is who you are becoming as an example to others.

We lead out of who we are, whether we like it or not. You can't create around you what doesn't exist within you; you will always create around you what exists within you. As Jesus said:

> You will recognize them by their fruits. Are grapes gathered from thornbushes, or figs from thistles? So, every healthy tree bears good fruit, but the diseased tree bears bad fruit. A healthy tree cannot bear bad fruit, nor can a diseased tree bear good fruit. Every tree that does not bear good fruit is cut down and thrown into the fire. Thus you will recognize them by their fruits. —Matthew 7:16-20 (ESV)

You can't foster a heart of peace in others if you don't have peace yourself. You can't help people become deeply formed by Christ if you are not deeply formed. You can't show others the way of

---

8   Edwin H. Friedman, *Failure of Nerve: Leadership in the Age of the Quick Fix* (New York, NY: Church Publishing Inc., 2017.)

love if you have not learned the way of love, and you can't teach others to pray if you are not growing in prayer.

My intention is not to overwhelm you as a growing leader, but I do recognize you could be feeling that way right now. Many of us are more likely to think too little of ourselves than too much. I am not claiming that you need to be perfect or to have "arrived" in some way to lead effectively. I am simply stating that, as leaders, we must be growing as examples.

This is why Christian leadership is the most challenging leadership context. Is leading in a church or faith-based organization harder? Yes. Why? Because who we are matters more. Because it's fundamentally not about getting things done but about the formation of people. This demands leaders in this context to be people who have been formed and are constantly being formed into Christ's likeness.

Growing in Christlikeness is our number one way to growing in effectiveness as a leader. It's easy to fall into the trap of thinking leadership is about technique. It's true that if you learn a few techniques and put them into practice, you will probably experience some short-term wins. And we will also discuss some helpful techniques later on in this book. But if they are not an overflow or expression of a life that's an example, they ultimately won't bear the fruit of Christlikeness in other people's lives. We might get some great stuff accomplished, but we won't help people grow in the ways that matter most.

"Leadership means going further than those one is leading."[9] "Christian leaders today need to model generosity in their giving,

---

9   H. G. Williamson, *Word Biblical Commentaries: Ezra-Nehemiah* (Grand Rapids, MI: Zondervan Academic, 1985) 246.

so that the average church-goer, whose offerings prove paltry in comparison, can see that greater sacrifice is both possible and necessary."[10]

We need to model sacrifice, love, diligence, spiritual practice, and peace. Why? Because it's highly unlikely that the people will grow beyond the pace and tone the leader sets; if they want to, they will most likely need to find a new leader.

I mentioned in chapter 1 that I have battled feelings of insecurity and feeling unqualified for most of my leadership journey. Becoming a pastor at the young age of twenty-five didn't help. But I take great confidence from Paul's encouragement to Timothy found in 1 Timothy 4:12.

How do I effectively lead others of all ages and stages? I set an example. I don't have to have arrived; I just need to be on the journey. The journey often involves repentance, apologies, resilience, and discipline. If we commit to the journey, our leadership will exponentially grow in effectiveness.

That's why the journey to being a great leader begins with being a great follower. We cannot form in others great followership if we have not learned it ourselves. This is about learning to be a great follower of Jesus and also a great follower of those God has placed over us in leadership. I served my lead pastor faithfully for many years before I became a lead pastor. And now, as a lead pastor, I still intentionally submit myself to the leadership of others so that I continue fostering a heart of followership at all times. We never grow or graduate beyond followership; it's a heart we must constantly foster. Jesus said:

---

[10] Craig L Blomberg, *Neither Poverty nor Riches: A Biblical Theology of Material Possessions* (Downers Grove, IL: InterVarsity Press, 1999) 55.

> "But among you it will be different. Whoever wants to be a leader among you must be your servant, and whoever wants to be first among you must become your slave. For even the Son of Man came not to be served but to serve others and to give his life as a ransom for many."
> —Matthew 20:26-28 (NLT)

Let's be honest: we want to be in charge. It's why the primary sin in most of our lives is often self-reliance. We want to be in control, and sometimes, our desire to lead can be because we want to call the shots. However, the invitation to Christian leadership always has service at its core, and that means first being a good follower.

Five Areas in Which to Grow As an Example

Next, let's unpack the five areas listed in 1 Timothy 4:12 in which Paul encouraged Timothy to grow as an example: in speech, in conduct, in love, in faith, and in purity.

Our speech is how others hear us.
Our conduct is how others see us.
Our love is how others experience us.
Our faith is how we trust God.
Our purity is the state of our internal world.

Growing As Examples of Speech

> "The tongue can bring death or life; those who love to talk will reap the consequences." —Proverbs 18:21 (NLT)

> "Kind words are like honey—sweet to the soul and healthy for the body". —**Proverbs 16:24 (NLT)**

> "Indeed, we all make many mistakes. For if we could control our tongues, we would be perfect and could also control ourselves in every other way." —**James 3:2 (NLT)**

Our words reveal the location of our lives. Jesus explained that from the overflow of the heart the mouth speaks (see Luke 6:45). How we speak about ourselves, others, and situations is a great revealer of where we are at in our lives and what's going on in our hearts and minds. Learning to view our words as indicators of the places in our heart that need God's grace and transformation is an important part of growing as an example.

Harnessing the power of speech to lead to transformation is powerful. Learning to bless people who curse us and celebrate people who we feel threatened by can shift our hearts to godly and fruitful places.

> **How you do anything is how you do everything.**

Growing As Examples of Conduct

How you do anything is how you do everything.

We can't compartmentalize our lives if we want to live with integrity. Our conduct, both the seen and unseen, in the ordinary and the spectacular, matters. We must learn to conduct ourselves well in the basics of life, under pressure, when people are watching, and when people are not. This includes how we do business, the time we turn up for work, and the diligence we display in our jobs to how we manage our finances, speak to our spouse, and take care of the things God has entrusted to us.

The Holy Spirit wants to help us and prompt us to be people who conduct ourselves with integrity in all areas of life in order to be examples to others. After washing the feet of His disciples, Jesus said, "I have given you an example to follow. Do as I have done to you" (John 13:15, NLT). The apostle Paul wrote to the Philippian church, "Keep putting into practice all you learned and received from me—everything you heard from me and saw me doing. Then the God of peace will be with you" (Philippians 4:9, NLT). Peter advised church leaders by writing, "Don't lord it over the people assigned to your care, but lead them by your own good example" (1 Peter 5:3, NLT).

Growing Examples of Love

How we relate to people matters. Transformed ways of relating to others are where our faith should show up. In the Sermon on the Mount, Jesus starts by teaching about how the kingdom of God transforms the way we treat each other.

Paul also defined this when writing about love in 1 Corinthians 13. He set up his description of love by writing that if what we do doesn't come from a heart of love, it doesn't count for anything as far as Heaven is concerned. This is a sober reminder to make sure we live as examples and not just give grand gestures or use techniques. Paul told them:

> Love is patient and kind; love does not envy or boast; it is not arrogant or rude. It does not insist on its own way; it is not irritable or resentful; it does not rejoice at wrongdoing, but rejoices with the truth. Love bears all things, believes all things, hopes all things, endures all things.
> —1 Corinthians 13:4-7 (ESV)

Growing in examples of love means growing in love in our relationships. To love is to want the best for another. We can only love well when we know God's love for us; only people who are loved well can truly love others well.

Start by growing in the relationships that are closest to you, and grow outwards from there. Think about how we live out our singleness or married lives. Our family relationships with children, parents, and siblings. How we relate to our brothers and sisters in Christ within His church. How we relate to friends and how we relate to acquaintances. Growing in love should impact all of these areas for the better.

Growing As Examples of Purity

Purity begins in our internal world and is revealed by our actions in our external world. Purity is about being one thing. Pure water doesn't have toxins, pure gold doesn't contain dross, and pure air doesn't have pollutants. As Christians, being pure is about being loyal to God and having our heart set on following Him. It's about Him ruling our internal world. Purity means that we are not divided between many cares and distractions. We are single-minded. When we live this way—from the inside out—it helps us to set our minds and our actions on the right things. It helps us run from temptation and not become defiled by the things of this world. We grow in purity through surrendering to God, putting Him first above all else and living from that place first in our hidden world.

Growing As Examples of Faith

Ultimately, everything flows from our relationship with God. Growing as examples of faith is about growing in the way we trust God with our lives. It's growing in our spiritual practices, which foster intimacy and trust. It's moving beyond having a quiet time with God in the morning and then going on living your life for the rest of the day. It's learning to rely on God in everything and integrate faith as a holistic way of living. Fight the pull to compartmentalize your life—with faith and church over here, and "real life" is over there. We grow in faith by seeing all of life as an arena in which Jesus can disciple us. It's learning to be with God and live out of that.

> # Fight the pull to compartmentalize your life—with faith and church over here, and "real life" is over there.

The key is our spiritual practices. There are many different types of ancient and modern spiritual practices that help us. From reading and meditating on God's Word to different types of prayer. Fasting, solitude, and silence. Embracing, noticing, developing a "rule of life," confessing, repenting, and accepting.

Sabbath and rest. We don't have time to cover them in detail here, but find some resources on spiritual practices and give some new ones a try (see Appendix 1). You'll see how spiritual practices grow your life of faith.

Another dimension of being an example of faith and leading from faith is not letting what we can see in the natural determine our level of expectation. In leadership, things often don't go well—it isn't always from strength to strength but from weakness to setback!

> "Now faith is confidence in what we hope for and assurance about what we do not see." —Hebrews 11:1 (NIV)

> "So faith comes from hearing, that is, hearing the Good News about Christ." —Romans 10:17 (NLT)

Hebrews 11 recounts all the amazing things accomplished by God in people's lives through faith. While it's the initial word of the good news of Christ that births faith to begin with, it's God's continual word that gives rise to faith for different circumstances. Peter was able to engage his faith to walk on water because Jesus told him to "come" and walk on it (see Matthew 14:29). We need to know God's Word generally as well as hear it specifically for different people and situations we are leading. When this happens, we are able to engage our faith as a response to God's revelation to us and begin to pray and walk in faith, so God can do supernaturally what we could never do naturally.

I find myself needing to grow in faith with every passing year. I find myself going to God first. I find myself more in prayer.

As this happens, we see God do the supernatural more often. Whether it is breakthrough in mission, healing, recruitment, church planting, or difficult situations, don't forget to lead in faith.

Growing as examples is where the true increase in the capacity of our churches and organizations for kingdom impact will come from. Often in my leadership, I've focused too much on our organizational or operational capacity. What do we have the ability to pull off? How many people can we attract? How big can we make this thing? But if our operational capacity exceeds our discipleship capacity—that is, our ability to make disciples and teach them to live in the way of Christ—it's all wasted energy. We are just growing a crowd or a service, not truly seeing God's church grow. By growing as examples of Christlikeness, we are growing in our discipleship capacity and, therefore, in our potential to create long-lasting kingdom impact.

To Lead is Good.
To Lead Is to Be an Example.

Put This Into Practice

Spiritual practices are the breeding ground of Christlikeness. They are where we take off the old person and put on the new. They are how we make ourselves available to the Spirit of God to change us, sanctify us, and lead us.

Here are practices every leader should be practicing (also refer to Appendix 1):

Daily Practices:
- Prayer—morning, midday, and evening.

- Reading and reflecting on the Word of God—it's not about how much you read but how much the Word gets into you. Read less, and reflect more.
- Solitude and silence—breathe deeply and slowly; make yourself available to God, even if it's just for ten minutes. Turn your phone off, find a quiet space, and every time your mind wanders, pray, "Here I am, God."

Weekly practices:
- Memorize scripture—pick a verse each week to memorize.
- Community—gather with smaller groups of believers in Jesus's name for fellowship.
- Worship and communion—gather with your local church to worship God and partake in communion.
- Sabbath rest—enjoy a day of just being with God; cease work (both paid and unpaid) and be present.
- Generosity—honor the Lord with the increase with which He has blessed your life, responding to others" needs and opportunities.

chapter 3

to lead is to pray

"No man is greater than his prayer life. The pastor who is not praying is playing; the people who are not praying are straying. We have many organizers, but few agonizers; many players and payers, few pray-ers; many singers, few clingers; lots of pastors, few wrestlers; many fears, few tears; much fashion, little passion; many interferers, few intercessors; many writers, but few fighters. Failing here, we fail everywhere."
—Leonard Ravenhill[11]

I had a neighbor who had this tree on our boundary. It was the worst tree I had ever seen. It grew fast, dropped its massive leaves twice a year, and produced strange flowers in between. I

---

11 Leonard Ravenhill, *Why Revival Tarries* (Bloomington, MN: Bethany House Publishers, 2004) 25.

always had to clean up the mess that this tree created all over our backyard. I constantly trimmed it and had to take all the waste to the landfill. My neighbor never wanted to prune it, never maintained it, and got annoyed when I cut it along the boundary line. Oh, and did I mention it was UGLY?

After twelve years, I was completely over it. Instead of chopping it down, I started researching how to poison the thing! I know. Just being real—we all reach our limits at some point, right? However, in the midst of my frustration, a thought came into my mind: *Why don't you pray to God and ask Him to get rid of the tree?* I know it seems crazy, but I couldn't shake off this thought. So, instead of buying poison, I prayed. I even laid hands on the tree! I prayed that it would either shrivel up and die (Jesus's style) or that it would be cut down and removed. Two weeks later, our family returned home from a couple of days away and were trying to figure out why our backyard looked so different.

I couldn't believe it. The tree was gone! PRAISE JESUS.

It turned out that one of our other neighbors had hired an arborist to deal with some of their own trees and had offered to take care of this one as well. As you can imagine, I was grateful to God, amazed by the power of prayer, and wondered why I didn't pray for the tree twelve years earlier!

Prayer Creates Change

The more I commit myself to prayer as a leader, the greater impact I seem to make. I have turned to God in ordinary times and in desperate times and have seen God do miracles in me, around me, and in the people I lead. I have seen cultures shift, marriages restored, children saved, and breakthrough occurs. I have seen

God answer my prayers by bringing the right people along at the right time. And I have also seen Him move people on to other things at the right time.

Godly leaders pray. It doesn't sound glamorous—not like the image we often have in our head of what a leader looks like. Someone at the front, someone outspoken, someone in charge, or someone oozing with confidence. Those things have their place, but prayer is an essential ingredient when it comes to leadership.

> **It doesn't matter in which sphere you lead or how many people you lead; prayer matters, and it makes a difference. Always.**

It doesn't matter in which sphere you lead or how many people you lead; prayer matters, and it makes a difference. Always.

As Jesus is our ultimate example of how to lead, let's begin by looking at His life and prayer habits. We know that He took time regularly to be on His own and pray. We know that He prayed when He was around His disciples because they asked Him to teach them how to pray. We see Jesus praying when He raised Lazarus from the dead. Jesus said that some miracles can only happen through prayer. Jesus asked His disciples to pray with Him and for Him before His arrest and crucifixion. He prayed that Peter's faith would not fail, and even after Peter ran away and denied Jesus, Peter stepped up and began to lead. Jesus prayed that His disciples would be kept safe in Him and endure what was to come. And He prayed that the church would be united.

Jesus's leadership was saturated in prayer.

So, why does prayer matter in leadership? Here are seven thoughts for you to consider:

Prayer Is How We Commune With God

It's taking time to be in and build a relationship. Healthy relationships require times of communication. Prayer is an ancient pathway of conversation with an attentive God who loves to listen and is poised to speak. If I were in proximity to my wife, but we didn't speak for a week, our relationship would be restricted and strained. Conversation is one of the ways that intimacy is built. Prayer is both mysterious and practical at the same time. Do you want to feel closer to God? Give Him more attention, and spend more time in conversation with Him.

Prayer Is How We Depend on God

Living by faith is about living in God-dependence—being God-reliant rather than self-reliant. Every time we pray to our Heavenly Father, we posture ourselves in dependence. We acknowledge that we want and need God. When we pray according to His pattern, which is revealed through the Lord's Prayer in Matthew 6:9-13 (ESV), we grow in greater dependence:

"Our Father in heaven,
    hallowed be your name."
        God would you be worshiped—by me and everyone else?
"Your kingdom come,
    your will be done, on earth as it is in heaven."

It's all about your kingdom, your plans, and your will above all else. I surrender my kingdom to yours and ask you to have your way.

"Give us this day our daily bread."

Everything I have comes from you; I may have a full pantry, but I recognize that you are my source. I'm leaning on you for provision, wisdom, and courage each day.

"And forgive us our debts,
     as we also have forgiven our debtors."

Thank you for overlooking all of my shortcomings, sins, and offenses. Because you have done that for me, I can find the will and the way to do that for others.

"And lead us not into temptation, but deliver us from evil."

I recognize the world is more than broken; there is real evil at work against you and me—lead me away from it, and protect me from its schemes.

"Yours is the kingdom and glory forever and ever, amen."

I'm aligning my life with what will last.

Prayer Is How God Aligns Us

Prayer is more about God's transforming us than our getting God to do something for us. When we reduce prayer down to a shopping list, we miss the point. Many people think of God as a genie; if you can rub Him the right way with the right words, you can get your three wishes. This perspective is formed more by our consumer culture than the way God has revealed Himself to us in Jesus and the Bible. People often say prayer is powerful (and it is), but it's most potent in its ability to transform us, to mold us, and to change us.

Prayer aligns us with God's perspective, peace, ways, and thoughts. Incredible things happen when we, as leaders, pray for the people who lead us and for those we lead. God speaks to us and gives us guidance. Unity is formed. Spirits are aligned. Honor is given. Situations are resolved because they first got resolved in us.

The more time you spend in prayer, the more opportunity God has to equip and empower you to be the leader He wants you to be.

Prayer Invokes the Power of God

When we read about the great, mighty, and powerful leaders throughout church history, we can't escape the connection between the Holy Spirit's power and prayer. Read any biography or history of a great revivalist, apostolic leader, or minister, and you will discover a life of prayer. In leadership, we need the supernatural power of the Holy Spirit in us, on us, and through us. We might think we are just leading a small group or a team, and we don't really need the power of the Holy Spirit, but we couldn't be more wrong. We need Him *more*. Whole movements and revivals have been started in small groups. We need the supernatural power of God to break strongholds in people's lives, set people free, cause miracles, and release heaven-filled calling into hearts. This is only possible when the life of the leader becomes a life of prayer.

> In leadership, we need the supernatural power of the Holy Spirit in us, on us, and through us.

Prayer in the Secret Place Informs the Public Face

Jesus said that when we pray, we should go into a closet or a secret place, hidden from others. And when we do that, He will reward us (see Matthew 6:6). There's something about a person or leader who seeks God in the secret place that can't help but be made public by God. Our public face—for better or for worse—is prepared and shaped in the secret place of prayer.

Prayer Is One of the Ways We Honor Those Leading Us

Unity is fostered when we pray for those that lead us. Psalm 133 teaches us that where there is unity, God commands a blessing. Praying for each other, including the people that lead us, is a powerful force that keeps us together and united in thought and heart. Paul asked those he led in Corinth to pray for him: "You also must help us by prayer, so that many will give thanks on our behalf for the blessing granted us through the prayers of many" (2 Corinthians 1:11, ESV).

Pray for your pastors and leaders.

Prayer Is One of the Ways We Serve the People We Lead

When we read the New Testament letters, we see a theme: Paul was always praying for the people he was leading. When we pray, things change in the lives of the people around us. If leaders would spend more time in prayer, they would spend less time having to solve problems.

There's also something powerful about knowing that people are actually praying for you! Knowing that people are praying for you makes you feel valued, spiritually led, and covered. It adds to your sense of connection and makes it more than just a relationship—it's a God-centered friendship.

Spending time each day praying—by name—for the people you lead is a transformative habit for all leaders.

> "I do not cease to give thanks for you, remembering you in my prayers."
> —Ephesians 1:16 (ESV)

> "I thank my God in all my remembrance of you, always in every prayer of mine for you all making my prayer with joy." —Philippians 1:3-4 (ESV)

What an amazing example for us to follow regarding the people we lead: not ceasing to give thanks and remembering those we are leading in joyful prayer.

When we pray, God often speaks. And we are able to access the superpower of the leader, the Holy Spirit. The Spirit can lay people on our heart, can show us what to pray for, and can give us heavenly ideas and solutions. The Spirit can give us wisdom and prophetic insight that can unlock the people and circumstances to which we bring leadership.

There have been many circumstances where the "interruption" of the Holy Spirit has birthed something new and profound that could never come about purely through human effort. In fact, this is really the story of our church. While I'm writing this, I'm on a flight to the funeral of a good friend who was a prophetic voice in our lives and church. The first time we met many years ago, he picked Katie and me out of a small meeting of which we were a part and began to speak about what God wanted to do through us and the church we were pastoring.

At that point, the church was tiny, limping along, and just trying to survive. But through the power of the Spirit, he spoke to the growth and people that would be raised up through it—the many people who would be saved. What was birthed by the Spirit that day began to break out almost immediately in the church, and over the next few years, we experienced an outpouring of God, many salvations, and significant growth.

Hearing the Spirit and responding to Him need to become a leader's normal mode of operation—from speaking prophetically into people's lives and situations to following through on even the most left-field promotions that need faith and obedience. These easy-to-overlook moments can often be the catalyst of breakthrough among the people we lead.

When we commit to being leaders who pray, we become people who can be led by the Spirit of God. Learning to hear His voice and abide in His presence are the training grounds for growing sensitivity to the Spirit's leading. There's a lot of art to leadership, but the Spirit's leading has the ability to trump it all in our lives. Pray, listen, and obey.

> To Lead is Good.
> To Lead is to Be an Example.
> To Lead is to Pray.

Put This Into Practice

Here are some prayers from the Bible that you can use to guide your *prayers for others*. Let these help you know what to pray for and how to pray.

A Prayer of Thanks

> "First, I thank my God through Jesus Christ for all of you, because your faith is proclaimed in all the world." —Romans 1:8 (ESV)

I thank You, God, through Your Son, Jesus Christ for _____ because _____. Amen.

A Prayer for Wisdom, Revelation, Knowledge, and Hope

> "I do not cease to give thanks for you, remembering you in my prayers, that the God of our Lord Jesus Christ, the Father of glory, may give you the Spirit of wisdom and of revelation in the knowledge of him, having the eyes of your hearts enlightened, that you may know what is the hope to which he has called you, what are the riches of his glorious inheritance in the saints, and what is the immeasurable greatness of his power toward us who believe, according to the working of his great might." —Ephesians 1:16-19 (ESV)

I pray that You, Heavenly Father, would give _____ a spirit of wisdom and of revelation in the knowledge of Jesus. Please enlighten _____'s heart that they would know what is the hope to which You have called them, the riches of Your glorious inheritance in the saints, and the immeasurable greatness of Your power towards _____ and all who believe according to the working of Your great might in Jesus. Amen.

A Prayer for Love, Discernment, and Righteousness

> "And it is my prayer that your love may abound more and more, with knowledge and all discernment, so that you may approve what is excellent, and so be pure and blameless for the day of Christ, filled with the fruit of righteousness that comes through Jesus Christ, to the glory and praise of God." —Philippians 1:9-11 (ESV)

> *Heavenly Father, I pray for _____, that their love may abound more and more, with knowledge and all discernment, so that they may know what is excellent, and so be pure and blameless for the day of Your coming, filled with the fruit of the righteousness that comes from You through Jesus Christ, to the glory and praise of God. Amen.*

A Prayer for Wisdom, Strength, Power, Endurance, Patience, and Joy

> "And so, from the day we heard, we have not ceased to pray for you, asking that you may be filled with the knowledge of his will in all spiritual wisdom and understanding, so as to walk in a manner worthy of the Lord, fully pleasing to him: bearing fruit in every good work and increasing in the knowledge of God; being strengthened with all power, according to his glorious might, for all endurance and patience with joy; giving thanks to the Father, who has qualified you to share in the inheritance of the saints in light." —Colossians 1:9-12 (ESV)

> *Heavenly Father, I pray for _____. Fill them with knowledge of Your will and spiritual*

wisdom and understanding, so they would walk in a manner worthy of You and fully pleasing to you. Would _____ bear fruit in every good work and constantly increase in their knowledge of You. As this happens, would _____ be strengthened with all Your power according to Your glorious might. Give them endurance and patience with joy as they thank You for what You have done in their life. Amen.

A Prayer for Calling, Purpose, and Good Works

> "To this end we always pray for you, that our God may make you worthy of his calling and may fulfill every resolve for good and every work of faith by his power, so that the name of our Lord Jesus may be glorified in you, and you in him, according to the grace of our God and the Lord Jesus Christ." —2 Thessalonians 1:11-12 (ESV)

Heavenly Father, I pray that You would make _____ worthy of their calling from You. May You fulfill their desire to do good and fulfill every work of faith by Your power. All of this I pray so that the name of Your Son, Jesus, would be glorified in _____ and _____ would be gloried in You according to the grace of our God and the Lord Jesus Christ. Amen.

A Prayer for the Effective Sharing of Our Faith

> "I pray that the sharing of your faith may become effective for the full knowledge of every good thing that is in us for the sake of Christ."
> —Philemon 1:6 (ESV)

Heavenly Father, I pray for _____ that the sharing of their faith would become effective for the full knowledge of every good thing that is in us for the sake of Christ. Amen.

A Prayer of Blessing

> "Beloved, I pray that all may go well with you and that you may be in good health, as it goes well with your soul." —3 John 1:2 (ESV)

Heavenly Father, I pray for _____ that it would go well with them and they would be in good health as it goes well with their soul. Would You bless them with health from the inside out in all things? Amen.

chapter 4

to lead is to grow in the word

"The cost of discipleship though it may take all we have, is small when compared to the lot of those who don't accept Christ's invitation to be a part of his company in the Way of life."
—Dallas Willard[12]

The day I turned seventeen, I left home and moved to a different city. I had recently become a follower of Jesus and wasn't sure what I wanted to do with my life. I reasoned that if the gospel really was the good news of the kingdom of God

---

[12] Dallas Willard, *The Spirit of the Disciplines: Understanding How God Changes Lives* (San Francisco, CA: HarperOne, 1988) 2.

becoming available to anyone through Jesus, then I should really learn more about it.

I hadn't grown up in church; I wasn't familiar with the Testaments, Bible stories, or Bible history. So, I went to Bible college. I was the youngest, by far. I was still growing up, I was out of my depth, and I played too much Minesweeper (if you know, you know) during lectures. During these lectures, I often had flashbacks to mathematics classes during high school, wondering when I would ever use or need algebra in my real life.

Although I was still trying to discover my specific calling and God-given purpose, I definitely knew that I wanted to serve God. However, I struggled at that time to see how much of what I was learning was going to help with that! Learning about hermeneutics, systematic theology, and Christology seemed disconnected from a life of ministry or leadership. Studying the Bible, book by book, seemed tedious and irrelevant as did analyzing word definitions in the Greek and Hebrew.

What the seventeen-year-old me failed to grasp was that understanding the Bible—having robust theology and an appreciation and context for church history—would have *everything* to do with leading.

A Thorough Grasp of the Word

Understanding the Bible, being able to teach it to others, and holding on to orthodoxy are inseparable from growing in leadership. We see this in the lives of Jesus, Paul, Peter, and any of the New Testament leaders into which we gain insight.

Jesus knew the Scriptures thoroughly. We can deduce that He had spent His childhood learning the Torah like all Jewish boys of His time. They were not able to carry around Bibles like we can or look up Bible verses on Google. Scrolls were bulky and precious and were stored at the local synagogue. They would spend time reading them and memorizing them.

Jesus was able to locate individual scriptures easily. Think about when He opened the scroll of Isaiah and declared the time of the Lord's favor (see Luke 4:18-19). He was able to quote scriptures to the devil in the midst of temptation, and He was able to unpack them in the Sermon on the Mount. He had an understanding even from an early age—far beyond His years. At the age of twelve, His questions and answers astounded the people.

The apostle Paul, who contributed significantly to the New Testament, was trained under Rabbi Gamaliel and had an expert understanding of the Old Testament. John the fisherman would go on to be as Scripture-saturated as anyone. His complex gospel is filled with inspired parallelism to the Old Testament, and the book of Revelation, which only has 404 verses, contains over five hundred references and illusions to Old Testament scriptures without a single quote.

The great Christian leaders of the ages all had a robust understanding of, appreciation toward, and respect for Scripture, from Augustine to Martin Luther, C. S. Lewis to Dwight Moody, Charles Spurgeon to Dallas Willard. You might be thinking, *Well, that's fine for the revivalists, the pastors, the church fathers, or those with a passion or brain for theology. I'm just a small group leader,* or *I'm just a team leader. I'm just discipling someone or caring for someone. What does this have to do with me?* It has everything to do with you; being able to understand the Bible and teach it is essential to being a godly leader.

> ## You live and lead from your theology—whether you realize it or not.

You live from your theology—whether you realize it or not.

You lead from your theology—whether you realize it or not.

All of us are living according to a script; we are living out of stories, ideologies, and philosophies. They shape our worldview although they often aren't coherent or even complete; they are a collection of different assumptions and things we have come to believe are true and right or ought to be. We may not be able to articulate them well, but we are living out of them. Our lives reveal them—what we think of life, the purpose of life, and what's truly important. Our worldview can be seen by what we spend money on and what we don't, how we prioritize our time, and what we sacrifice and for what. It can be seen by how we relate, with whom we spend time, and what we read and watch.

The world has immensely ramped up its ability to be a formational force in our lives over the last couple of decades. Our educational institutions, as well as media in all forms, have greater access to our lives, time, minds, and souls than ever before. Even back in the 1950s, some Christians used to fear the TV and its formational effect. Preachers have long warned about the ideologies and value systems overtly and subtly peddled through many and most programs. If you add up the amount of time a child spends at school, in front of a TV, and on a device, you are talking about hours and hours of formation every week. When you compare that to the amount of time that they might be engaged in Jesus-centered conversation, in the Word, in church, or in prayer, it's cause for great alarm and concern.

Christians are statistically and typically spending less time with their church community and are less regular with and less engaged in spiritual practices now than in the past.[13] We spend ten minutes with God in the morning, but we spend two hours on our phone scrolling or watching Netflix—probably both. We are highly unlikely to be forming a truly Jesus-centered, truth-saturated, godly worldview with such habits. Growing in our knowledge of the Word, time in the Word, understanding of the Word, and memorization of the Word is essential to Christlike transformation in our lives and leadership.

What you accept, what you expect, what you tolerate, and what you say are all shaped by your current theology. Sadly, many in the body of Christ have separated leadership from the ability to teach. Worldly analogies of what it means to lead are used rather than Scripture and examples from the life of Jesus. You don't have to be a theologian to be a leader, but you do need to love the Word and intentionally and continually grow in it.

Grow in the Word and Watch Your Leadership Grow Too

My advice to leaders is to spend more time growing in your theology than your leadership, and watch how your leadership grows as a result! The Word gives our life an authority and stability from above. The Word is what never returns void. The Word is what

---

13 "A New Chapter in Millennial Church Attendance," *Barna Group*, 4 Aug. 2022, www.barna.com/research/church-attendance-2022/.

gives the opportunity for faith to be birthed. The Word is strong. The Word is alive. The Word is active. The Word remains. And the great news, especially for volunteer leaders that may not have too much time, is that there are many tools and resources available to help us grow in this area (see Appendix 2).

The following is a biblical description of the qualifications of deacons, who would be the equivalent of small group leaders and team leaders in the church today: "They must hold the mystery of the faith with a clear conscience" (1 Timothy 3:9, ESV). To do this, they must know the Word of God and be committed to its truth; they cannot be shallow in their faith or taken in by false doctrine. And to be clear: it doesn't mean you need to be able to teach. That is a qualification for elders, not deacons. But you do need to know the Word and lead out of that.

Today's abundant access to teaching presents unique challenges for the body of Christ. If Paul said to the Corinthian Christians that they had many teachers but only one Father, how much more true would that be for many Christians today? Between Christian television, podcasts, Instagram influencers, and YouTube channels, it's no wonder many are confused or conflicted.

There's no lack of content, but there is a lack of understanding, a lack of growth, a lack of wisdom, and a lack of consistency.

> **There's no lack of content, but there is a lack of understanding, a lack of growth, a lack of wisdom, and a lack of consistency.**

As a leader, it's important to physically sit under the teaching of the local church you are a part of and have that as the primary way your theology is shaped. Your local pastor, eldership, and leadership team have been entrusted with feeding the sheep in their care. Jesus said that a prophet is not honored in his hometown (see Matthew 13:57). But this doesn't have to be the case and shouldn't be the Christian way. We are called to honor one another. Unfortunately, in a time in which you can listen to both the greatest and the weirdest from all over the world, we can often undervalue the person God has actually sent to care for us—the leader who is praying for us and actually thinking about us when they prepare their teaching sermons.

We see Paul write to Timothy about the importance of reading and teaching Scripture (which requires understanding). Timothy was commissioned in his leadership to "keep a close watch on yourself and on the teaching. Persist in this, for by doing so you will save both yourself and your hearers" (1 Timothy 4:16, ESV). As leaders, we want to be a conduit of doctrinally sound orthodox teaching of our local church, fulfilling 2 Timothy 2:2 (ESV), which says: "What you have heard from me in the presence of many witnesses [not the random stuff said among friends] entrust to faithful men, who will be able to teach others also."

One of the big shifts in Western culture over the last seventy years is the moral shift. Seventy years ago, the common moral framework through which Westerners viewed the world was highly aligned with God's moral framework regarding the following issues in no particular order: divorce, sex and children outside of wedlock, sexual orientation, acceptable language, and wholesome entertainment. These would have all been viewed very similarly by a fair majority of people whether or not they were Christian. However, as time has gone on, we can no longer take for granted that we are in agreement on every moral doctrine. Add the shift in cultural understanding with the digital age and social media in which everyone can peddle their agenda, and followers of Jesus can often be left confused and with piecemeal theology.

As rational thinking seems to be at an all-time low and emotional reactions at an all-time high, being of sober mind and saturated in the Word of God has never been more important.

Helping people align their lives with the revealed Word of God is one of the biggest challenges that volunteer leaders in church and faith-based organizations face. Being grounded in, growing in, and being a conduit for the teaching of the Word within our church matters more than ever. I'm noticing a shift even in my role as a shepherd and teacher/preacher. I'm having to spend less time giving inspiring preaching and more time getting back to basics—pull up a stool, teach more, and ensure we have solid understanding. Now, teaching and preaching are not mutually exclusive. In fact, the best messages involve both and move the heart and the mind by the power of the Holy Spirit.

Protecting People From Incorrect Theology and Heresy

So, how do we help protect people from incorrect theology and outright heresy? Here are two tips that I believe will help you:

Understand the Difference Between Bad Theology and Heresy

Saint Augustine is often quoted as saying, "In essentials, unity; in non-essentials, liberty; in all things, charity." Whether he or a lesser-known German Lutheran theologian did, the point is that it's not okay to believe whatever you want.[14] Paul spent significant time rebutting and rebuking heresy through his epistles. There is what we would call an orthodox understanding of the Christian faith. Peter, Paul, and others were preaching it after Jesus's ascension. They protected it in their writings. It's been canonized (collected) as the New Testament, summarized by the early church fathers, and passed on through generations to us.

The essentials can be best summed up in the creeds. The Nicene Creed adopted in 325 AD[15] is the oldest creed. While numerous versions are available, the following is from Marquette University:

> *We believe in one God, the Father, the Almighty, maker of heaven and earth, of all that is seen and unseen.*
>
> *We believe in one Lord, Jesus Christ, the only Son of God, eternally begotten of the Father, God from God, Light from Light, true God from true God, begotten not made, one in being with the Father. Through him all things were made. For us and for our salvation he came down from heaven; by the power of the Holy Spirit he was born of the Virgin Mary, and became man. For our sake he*

---

14 Mark Ross, "In Essentials Unity, in Non-Essentials Liberty, in All Things Charity," *Ligonier Ministries*, 1 Sept. 2009, www.ligonier.org/learn/articles/essentials-unity-non-essentials-liberty-all-things.
15 "Nicene Creeds," *Cordata Presbyterian Church*, 19 Nov. 2018, cordatachurch.org/adult-ministries/nicene-creeds.

was crucified under Pontius Pilate, he suffered, died, and was buried. On the third day he rose again in fulfillment of the Scriptures; he ascended into heaven and is seated at the right hand of the Father. He will come again in glory to judge the living and the dead, and his kingdom will have no end.

We believe in the Holy Spirit, the Lord, the giver of life, who proceeds from the Father and the Son. With the Father and the Son he is worshipped and glorified. He has spoken through the prophets.

We believe in one, holy, catholic, and apostolic Church.

We acknowledge one baptism for the forgiveness of sins.

We look for the resurrection of the dead, and the life of the world to come.

Amen.

If you want to know what the belief statement of your church should be, it's most likely this or one closely related to this. This has been the core belief statement of the church since its inception and has been written in this form for almost 1,700 years. There is no need to reinvent the wheel; this wheel has served the church well and will continue to do so!

> **There is no need to reinvent the wheel; this wheel has served the church well and will continue to do so!**

When it comes to these essential matters, we want to be in 100 percent unity; anything else is heresy. But in matters not covered by the creeds, we can have liberty to a certain degree. We can agree to disagree. We must also encourage sound reason and solid biblical scholarship and look for precedent in church history as we interpret Scripture. It is important to add here that we must interpret Scripture with the whole church, not just ourselves. They are "ours," not just "mine" or "yours." While there are a lot of gray areas, there are also a lot of black and white. I'm all about being receptive and teachable and having an open mind. The whole point in learning is to learn and then share what you have learned. Don't let the gray stop you from being convicted about the black and white.

Remember: the reason you open your mind is to close it again.

Encourage Orthodox Theology

We must be a presence in people's lives that keeps pointing them back to the Word of God. When people discuss the many situations and problems taking place in their lives, let's be the ones who ask the following questions:

- What does the Bible say about that option?
- Does the Bible support that way of thinking?
- What examples have you found in the Bible that can guide you to effectively navigate your situation?

When we are growing in the Word, we are growing in the grace and knowledge of Jesus. The Word never returns void and always accomplishes what it was sent forth to do (see Isaiah 55:11). When we grow in the Word, we grow in wisdom. Wisdom is doing the right thing in the right way in a particular situation.

The book of Proverbs explains the benefits of getting wisdom and the pitfalls in ignoring it:

> The fear of the Lord is the beginning of wisdom, and the knowledge of the Holy One is insight. —Proverbs 9:10 (ESV)

The Scriptures are God's revelation of Himself to us; they are how we grow in knowledge of the Holy One. When that happens from a heart posture of proper fear—that is, reverence and respect for God's supremacy—we will grow in wisdom. Fear, understood another way, is a lively sense of awe, wonder, and beauty that draws us in. Growing in wisdom is about learning to live in the Word as it actually is. It's about aligning with reality, and that's why aligning with the greatest reality (God) is central to learning to live in His Word.

> **We need wisdom. Not only will wisdom bless every part of your life, but it will also add depth, strength, and longevity to your leadership.**

We need wisdom. Not only will wisdom bless every part of your life, but it will also add depth, strength, and longevity to your leadership. We can become people who know how to do the right thing—in the right way—in any particular situation by fearing the Lord, growing in knowledge of His Word, and being led by His Spirit. This causes faith to be birthed and flourish. Read Jesus's interaction with the centurion soldier:

> When he had entered Capernaum, a centurion came forward to him, appealing to him, "Lord, my servant is lying paralyzed at home, suffering terribly." And he said to him, "I will come and heal him." But the centurion replied, "Lord, I am not worthy to have you come under my roof, but only say the word, and my servant will be healed. For I too am a man under authority, with soldiers under me. And I say to one, "Go," and he goes, and to another, "Come," and he comes, and to my servant, "Do this," and he does it." When Jesus heard this, he marveled and said to those who followed him, "Truly, I tell you, with no one in Israel have I found such faith." —**Matthew 8:5-10 (ESV)**

We learn something powerful about faith here: faith is about knowing how to be under authority. Faith is about learning to be under God's authority and operating in this world according to our Heavenly Father's will. Faith is something that is given to us by God as we respond to His Word. Faith is a response. When we grow strong in the Word and learn to live life under it, we often experience growth in our faith. When this happens, we will find ourselves taking more God-directed risks and experiencing ourselves among God's radical work.

When we begin to operate in new depths of faith in our leadership, what is possible is redefined. As my faith has grown as a leader, I've stepped out to pray for healing and have seen people healed. I have taken risks to plant churches, I've endured tough seasons, and I've experienced the fruit on the other side. I've been able to lead our church to buy property and continue to expand our ministry's impact. Most recently, God spoke to us about giving away a piece of land, which the church owned, to our indigenous Māori people as part of a reconciliation journey. It's a long story regarding why God might ask us to do something like that, but having the faith to trust Him would not have been possible if the Word of God wasn't my daily bread.

To Lead is Good.
To Lead is to Be an Example.
To Lead is to Pray.
To Lead is to Grow in the Word.

Put This Into Practice

1. We can read the Word daily for information by studying the Word and using Bible studying tools. This helps us shape a biblical worldview, growing in knowledge and understanding.
2. We can read the Word daily for inspiration by taking the Word in and being in tune with the promptings of the Holy Spirit who wants to use the Word to encourage us in our lives.
3. We can read the Word for intimacy by engaging in contemplative practices, such as Lectio Divina. This is a traditional monastic practice of scriptural reading, meditation, and prayer intended to help us become increasingly aware and connected to God's presence through the Scriptures.
    - The following Psalm not only sets the theme for the whole book of Psalms (which is about the God-dependent life contrasted with the self-dependent life), but it

gives great encouragement for us as leaders growing in our knowledge of the Word. It teaches us that if we love the Word, meditate on it, and allow ourselves to be molded by it, our lives will be secure and fruitful.

- Take time to study the Psalm below using commentaries and online Bible study tools.
- Read the Psalm over a few times and receive the encouragement the Spirit illuminates. Engage in *Lectio Divina*—still your mind for sixty seconds—practicing silence—read the Psalm slowly and out loud. Pause for thirty seconds and repeat, this time taking time to notice what the Spirit might be highlighting in the words. Begin to pray into these. Take time to contemplate. Read the Psalm one last time aloud slowly to finish.

Psalm 1 (ESV)

Blessed is the man
 who walks not in the counsel of the wicked,
 nor stands in the way of sinners,
 nor sits in the seat of scoffers;
 but his delight is in the law of the Lord,
 and on his law he meditates day and night.
He is like a tree
 planted by streams of water
 that yields its fruit in its season,
 and its leaf does not wither.
In all that he does, he prospers.
The wicked are not so,
 but are like chaff that the wind drives away.

Therefore the wicked will not stand in the judgment,
 nor sinners in the congregation of the righteous;
for the Lord knows the way of the righteous,
 but the way of the wicked will perish.

chapter 5

to lead is to trust

*"You can ignore the principles that govern trust—
but they will not ignore you."*
—Stephen Covey[16]

When I think of the teams that I have enjoyed being a part of the most, there has always been high trust, enabling us to accomplish tasks with joy and ease. Trust is the lifeblood of all relationships. There is a direct correlation between the trust within a relationship and its health. Trust determines our ability to lead and be led. Trust (or the lack of it) shapes our experience of leadership. Everything moves at the speed of trust.[17] Strong

---
16 Stephen M. R. Covey, "The Speed of Trust," *FranklinCovey*, www.speedoftrust.com/.
17 Stephen M. R. Covey, *The Speed of Trust: The One Thing that Changes Everything* (New York, NY: CoveyLink, 2006).

marriages, long-term friendships, and healthy churches and organizations are built on trust. Great small groups and effective teams only exist when trust is flowing and growing.

> Trust is the lifeblood of all relationships.

What Is Trust?

Trust is the firm belief in the reliability, truth, or ability of someone or something. Trust is so helpful that it allows us to not have to overthink everything and live on hyperalert. When trust isn't present, even with the basics of life, we become paranoid, obsessive, anxious, and crippled by fear.

In our everyday lives, trust is practiced subconsciously. Every time we sit on a chair without checking out its engineering specs and testing it with an object heavier than ourselves first, we are practicing trust.

Even so, we have all probably been witnesses to those unfortunate moments when someone's trust was misplaced, and the chair collapsed under the pressure. We drive and assume the brake pedal will allow us to stop. We order something online and give over our credit card details in good faith that the object will be sent, and our card won't be misused. We trust the Internet will work, our phone will receive messages, our power will stay connected, our wheels will stay on the car, our company will pay us, the train will go where it said it would, and the barista won't spit in our coffee. We trust this bread really is gluten-free, the painkiller will help, and the builder did a good job ensuring our ceiling won't fall on our head when we sleep. We practice trust every day.

While we practice trust thousands of times a day in so many areas of our life, trusting in our human relationships can be a challenge. A person who has experienced the unfortunate event of a chair collapsing under them normally becomes a little more vigilant when choosing a place to sit. They have misplaced their trust before and are now less likely to give it as freely next time. In our relationships, we are like that too. There wouldn't be a single one of us who hasn't been disappointed by someone before. From the trivial event of someone turning up late to the heartbreak of being betrayed in marriage, all of us have experienced our trust being broken. When we assumed someone would be reliable or truthful only to find they weren't, it makes us slow to trust again. And fair enough, it's this heightened sense of self-protection that keeps us safe and from being stuck in destructive relationship patterns.

Leading well in church or faith-based organizations seems to be an increasing challenge because of the way trust has been misused in the past. The stories of leaders who have abused trust circulate like wildfire while the majority of faithful, trustworthy pastors" stories don't get told. Many people coming into our churches have experienced broken trust or the trauma of leadership abuse. This means that when we are leading people, we are not starting from a place of assumed trust or trust neutrality. Instead, we are on the back foot. People are twice shy after being once bitten. As a leader, we have to earn people's trust more than ever and make sure we treasure it when we get it!

> **As a leader, we have to earn people's trust more than ever and make sure we treasure it when we get it!**

One of the challenges in leadership can be our transference of hurt, disappointment, and ultimately mistrust onto people who didn't break our trust at all. When we have had our trust broken enough times or in traumatic ways, we can begin to relate to everyone from a stance of mistrust. We see this especially when people trigger us or remind us of someone that broke our trust in the first place. This can often happen in church when people have had negative experiences in the past that haven't been properly dealt with, forgiven, reconciled, or healed. We might not be the leader who hurt them all those years ago, but we are treated as if we were. As a pastor, I'm never solely trusted purely on my own merits, integrity, safety, or faithfulness. I'm often touted or not through the lens of people's pain and past experiences.

I write all of this because if healthy relationships require high trust, then, as leaders, we need to do the following:
- Be aware of trust dynamics.
- Be people who are growing in our ability to trust.
- Be people who are growing in trustworthiness.

When the lack of trust in ourselves and others is not identified and resolved, we put a limit on our ability to lead and be led. Having honest conversations, practicing forgiveness, seeking healing, and risking again are all necessary steps in flowing and growing in trust.

Have Honest Conversations

When we are not speaking truthfully (and, of course, lovingly) to each other, trust is low. Think about these questions that act as the litmus test for trust:

- To what degree can you be honest about how you're feeling?
- Can you give and receive feedback?
- Can you give and receive correction?
- How much unsaid stuff is going on in this relationship?
- Is there a feeling of walking on eggshells or unspoken elephants in the room?

Being a leader is having the courage to say what others wouldn't, ask questions others wouldn't, and ensure the air is clear so trust can flow and grow.

Practice Forgiveness

To love is to make yourself vulnerable and, therefore, display trust. When you put yourself out there, there's always the possibility you will be hurt, misunderstood, rejected, or disappointed. Such is the nature of relationships. But there's also the possibility for a lifelong marriage, the joy and beauty of friendship, and the warm embrace of a spiritual family. When you're in relationship, it's not a matter of *if* you will get hurt but *when*. We are all human, and despite our best efforts at times, we find ourselves hurting those we love. So, for relationships to flourish, forgiveness must be practiced.

Forgiveness is not saying what they did was okay. God doesn't say our sin was no big deal. Jesus died for it on the cross—it's a big deal. It's saying, "I will no longer hold the offense against you." Repentance is when the person who committed the offense recognizes what they have done, expresses sorrow, and makes a commitment going forward to act differently. When forgiveness meets repentance, reconciliation occurs, and any trust that was broken can begin to be rebuilt. We will all have many times in life's journey when we need to give forgiveness and when we need to repent. It's the humbling and necessary journey of leadership.

Seek Healing

In the New Testament, when we read the word "saved," it's often the Greek word *sozo*, which carries with it the idea of wholeness. When Jesus saves us, He is not just speaking of making things right between Him and us, although it's certainly not less than that. He is saying that in Him, He is making us whole. That's why great theologians have often said we are saved, we are being saved, and we will be saved.

One of the areas God wants to see healed and whole in our lives is our heart. A healed heart finds it easy to trust, but a wounded one doesn't. If we are to be godly and effective leaders, pursuing healing and wholeness in past areas of relational pain isn't optional—it's a necessity. This often involves counseling, prayer, forgiveness, spiritual breakthrough, and vulnerable sharing. It can be messy, but mess always gives way to beauty and freedom.

> **If we are to be godly and effective leaders, pursuing healing and wholeness in past areas of relational pain isn't optional—it's a necessity.**

Risk Again

When every chair you have ever sat on feels like it collapses, we often come to the conclusion that it may be better to just stay standing. When we do that, the walls we once built to protect ourselves inevitably become our prison. By God's grace, we must open the gates and take the risk to love and trust again. As the great British poet Alfred Tennyson famously wrote, "'Tis better to have loved and lost than never to have loved at all." While love is risky—as it requires trust—it's worth it. This is how God loves, and it is the path we are invited to follow.

We live in a culture of growing distrust. People are increasingly skeptical of others. There's been enough corruption, corporate greed, and government betrayal to warrant a certain degree of skepticism. In the church, there have been local and high-profile moral failures. There are constant reports of abuses and enough church politics to disenfranchise the average person. Obviously, bad news travels faster than good, and it's paramount to remember that. The church helps hundreds of millions of people every day, and this trust must be tempered against cases of brokenness, abuse, betrayal, and corruption. I can understand why many people have a hard time trusting the church and church leaders specifically. Given the overall climate and number of first- or second-hand stories going around, it's no surprise we have some trust hurdles.

But beware the danger of cynicism. Cynicism is the posture of assuming the worst about people's motives. Trust and cynicism cannot coexist. Cynicism in being skeptical of others" motives only pollutes your own. It places you in judgment if you begin playing God and presuming you can see into the heart. It's a log that makes specks look out of proportion. Cynicism sneaks up on you, one thought and comment at a time. It reigns in your thoughts, slips out in gossip, and makes its full assault in sarcasm. As a leader, guard your heart against it, and don't let it take root and fester in your groups and teams.

Trust Needs to Flow in Several Directions

Trust Needs to Flow to Us

To thrive as a leader, we need to know we are trusted. If you are not feeling trusted with what you have been entrusted, it's time to have a chat with your leader. We thrive knowing someone believes in us and has our back. But be careful not to expect more trust than you have earned. There is a process to trust. Trust, to a degree, is assumed *and* given. Based on your performance, that trust is either confirmed, grown, or diminished. As you show yourself trustworthy over time, more trust will be granted. Don't be afraid to do the hard yards of proving yourself faithful. Don't be disappointed if you're not promoted or entrusted on your own timetable. Trust your leader.

When I am teaching my kids to drive, I don't throw them the keys for the first time and let them give it a go. They are too precious, others on the road are too precious, and the car is too precious. They first study to learn the road code and get their learner license. They get lessons from me in a controlled environment without other cars, such as a parking lot. When ready, we take the risk and head out to the open road, taking it slow and careful. Then, after a lot of practice, the types of roads and environments they can drive in grows.

In New Zealand, they can then go and sit their restricted license which allows them to drive on their own. They are able to take the car on their own every now and then. After another long period of practice and getting some miles under their belt, they sit their full license test and have the freedom to do as they wish (with their own car, of course). They have been trusted with more and more as they have grown in the ability to be entrusted. I would be a horrible and dangerous father if I threw them the keys on their first time in the driver's seat and left them to it. Trust and leadership work the same way.

Trust Needs to Flow From Us

Because everything moves at the speed of trust, we need to be trusting people—trusting our leaders, our pastors, and the people we lead. We need to model trust, give trust, practice trust, and entrust. In the same way you will thrive when trusted, so will your pastor, your team, and your group. While we might have to earn the trust of others, I believe we relate in a much healthier way when we approach every relationship with some freely given trust to get things started. We might find ourselves disappointed every now and then by starting from a trusting place, but the health it will create everywhere else will be more than worth it!

> **While we might have to earn the trust of others, I believe we relate in a much healthier way when we approach every relationship with some freely given trust to get things started.**

Trust Needs to Flow Around Us

We need to foster an atmosphere of trust in the groups and teams we lead by watching out for cynicism and confronting it for what it is. By doing this, we will create a safe place for honest conversations. We need to become people who model and encourage the giving and receiving of feedback well while leading others to forgiveness, repentance, and reconciliation. We should be encouraging people on their own healing journeys and cheering them on to risk again.

All of Us Can Foster Trust

In the book *Strength-Based Leadership*, the authors discuss the importance of trust.[18] According to surveys, the number one

---

[18] Tom Rath and Barrie Conchie, *Strengths Based Leadership: Great Leaders, Teams, and Why People Follow* (New York, NY: Gallup Press, 2008).

factor that determines people having a productive and healthy relationship with their company and boss is trust. They go on to show that this is good news because every personality type and strength profile can foster trust.

The book goes on to profile different leaders of highly successful companies. What's revealed is that they all go about leading very differently. The common thread, however, is that they are all good at developing trust. The highly relational leader develops trust by creating an environment of belonging and warmth. The highly visionary leader develops trust through inspiration and imagination. The executing leader develops trust by getting things done, and the strategic-thinking leader develops trust by solving problems and making improvements. The exciting thing is that for you, as the leader, it doesn't matter what your wiring is. You can leverage who you are to develop trust by playing to your strengths.

Everything moves at the speed of trust,[19] but when we are working on strengthening and developing trust, it doesn't feel like things are moving very fast at all. Sometimes, having the necessary conversations needed to develop trust might even feel like we are going backwards. It can feel messy when we honestly share our hurts, experiences, and reservations. These crucial conversations, however, are essential to building and rebuilding trust. Don't shy away from them; cover them in prayer, embrace them with grace, and get good at listening, forgiving, repenting, and changing.

How Do We Trust When There's a Gap?

Gaps are inevitable: gaps in understanding, gaps in information, and gaps in motive. Gaps exist in every relationship, and while,

---
19 Stephen M. R. Covey, *The Speed of Trust*.

as leaders, we can attempt to close the gaps that can be closed, we will never be able to close every gap. If my wife is running late to get home from somewhere, and she isn't answering her phone (very normal in our situation), it creates a gap. But it's my choice what I fill that gap with. I could think the worst: she's been in a car accident, she's having an affair, or she doesn't care about me. Or, I can fill it with the best: she's helping someone, she got caught in a significant conversation, or she's buying me a present.

Frontline leaders will experience gaps. They will also feel the frustration and anxiety of the gaps that the people they lead feel towards the whole church or organization. We need to foster an environment that seeks clarity and chooses to assume the best when the gaps appear.

When we have a deep sense of trust in God, it's easier to trust others. American theologian Marcus Borg, in his work *The Heart of Christianity: Rediscovering a Life of Faith*, looks to the Middle Ages and discovers there were four Latin words that were used to describe faith.[20] Faith in our modern world has mostly been reduced to believing the right things, but faith—as the ancients understood it—was much richer than that.

- Faith as assensus. This is giving your mental assent to the truth of a claim; faith as believing that something is true.[21]
- Faith as fidelitas. The central meaning of this word equates with fidelity. This is faith as faithfulness to God but not as faithfulness to certain statements about God. It is

---

[20] Marcus J. Borg, *The Heart of Christianity: Rediscovering a Life of Faith* (New York, NY: HarperCollins, 2003).
[21] Marcus J. Borg, *The Heart of Christianity: Rediscovering a Life of Faith*, 28.

faithfulness to your relationship with God. Think of marriage and one's commitment to each other.[22]
- Faith as fiducia. It's like the English word fiduciary but without the -ry at the end. The English equivalent of faith as fiducia is faith as trust.[23] This is faith as radical trust in God or, as it is attributed to Søren Kierkegaard: "Trust in the buoyancy of God."[24]
- Faith as visio. Faith that affects our whole way of seeing.[25]

As faith comes to mean more to us than just believing the right things, but rather entering a covenant relationship with God, we will experience a lowering of anxiety, a release from the need to control, and a freedom to walk in trust with people knowing it's ultimately God who is in control. We must remember that He is good, He is at work, and He is trustworthy.

> **God is good, He is at work, and He is trustworthy.**

To Lead is Good.
To Lead is to Be an Example.
To Lead is to Pray.
To Lead is to Grow in the Word.
To Lead is to Trust.

---

22 Marcus J .Borg, *The Heart of Christianity: Rediscovering a Life of Faith*, 34.
23 Marcus J .Borg, *The Heart of Christianity: Rediscovering a Life of Faith*, 31.
24 Marcus J .Borg, *The Heart of Christianity: Rediscovering a Life of Faith*, 31.
25 Marcus J .Borg, *The Heart of Christianity: Rediscovering a Life of Faith*, 34.

Put This Into Practice

Reflect on the following:
1. Do you feel trusted? Is there a conversation you need to have with those leading you?
2. Are you trustworthy? Can you be relied on to do what you say and choose to put others before yourself under pressure?
3. What crucial conversations need to be had to build or rebuild trust?
4. How can you build trust with those you lead?

chapter 6

to lead is to learn

"Leadership and Learning are Indispensable to each other."
—John F. Kennedy[26]

I recently caught up with one of my mentors. He is a lot older than me; however, my first unplanned question as we sat down was, "What are you learning at the moment?" It was then that I realized some of why I admire and trust him so much; he is a humble learner. And that makes him a safe and trustworthy leader.

When we step up to lead, we also must step up to be intentional learners. If we don't, we can set an unhelpful example for those we lead and unintentionally become their ceiling. The most

---

[26] John F. Kennedy, "Leadership and Learning: The Need for Constant Evolution," *Applied Corporate Governance*, 25 Apr. 2018, www.applied-corporate-governance.com/leadership-and-learning/#:~:text=In%20a%20speech%20to%20be,leaders%20to%20be%20constantly%20evolving.

important growth is the growth of the leader because, to tweak Craig Groeschel's Tweet from chapter 1, as leaders get better, everything gets better. Imagine six people standing in a single-file line. You, as the leader, are at the front. When you're learning (and, therefore, growing), you begin to walk further along the line, giving space for those behind you to walk. But if you stay still, they will stay still because there is no space for them to walk and grow for themselves. They will most likely go and find someone else to follow.

The point of this chapter is this: leaders are learners. There are many ways we can be intentional about learning, but they all have one paramount virtue at their core.

Leaders are learners.

The Most Pleasant of Virtues

I took a couple of my boys for a walk across the countryside to find some hidden beaches on a recent family camping trip. During the walk, we discussed what the greatest virtue is. Once I clarified the definition of virtue, one of my sons answered after a bit of deliberation with "love," and the other settled on "the fruit of the Spirit" (great pastor's kid). This led to an argument about who was right, which didn't display the virtue or fruit previously proposed. I interrupted them and offered to tell them what I think the greatest virtue is. They were curious, so I told them. Humility. They were confused. I further explained that without it, you cannot possess the other godly and noble virtues. It's the posture of humility that allows God—and others—to help form us into people of love and the other fruits of the Spirit. We cannot be formed without humility; we can only be broken.

> **We cannot be formed without humility; we can only be broken.**

C. S. Lewis said, "Humility, after the first shock, is a cheerful virtue."[27] Its initial shock is how it confronts our ego, leaving us feeling exposed and vulnerable. Its initial shock is how it challenges the familiar way we have been thinking and living. But that shock gives way to pleasantry. As our ego is put in its place, we experience the joy of dependence on God. Our vulnerability leads us to know God and to be formed by Him in a deeper way. Humility becomes the pathway to great reward as our softness allows for God's forming touch. Humility becomes a quiet confidence in our Lord and Savior, garnished with the appearance of the fruit of the Spirit in ever-increasing measure. Humility is the doorway to godliness.

It is only the humble leader who can truly be trusted to lead. The apostle Peter put it like this: "God opposes the proud but gives grace to the humble" (1 Peter 5:5, NLT).

The problem with pride is that it stands up against God. Pride says, "I already know, and I can do it on my own." Pride promotes the self to the position of God, and that's why God doesn't stand for it. Humility, in contrast, relates to the world as it really is.

---

27 C. S. Lewis, *The Problem of Pain* San Francisco, CA: HarperOne, 2009).

Humility recognizes the supremacy of God and the fragility of self. Humility creates space for God to be God in our lives and in the areas of our leadership. Humility and pride can be seen as space issues. When people appear proud, we say they are "full of themselves." When they appear humble, we say they are "empty of self." When we are empty, we are ready to be filled by God. There's space for Him. Now, that's exciting!

G. K. Chesterton was a great thinker and apologist. The thought in Chesterton's day, much like our day, was that a person should rule who feels they can rule. Chesterton wrote a rebuttal in response:

> *Whatever else is Christian, this is heathen. If our faith comments on government at all, its comment must be this—that the man should rule who does not think that he can rule. Heroes may say, "I will be king"; but the Christian saint must say, "Nolo episcopari." (The traditional formal refusal made by a cleric in the Roman Catholic and Anglican churches of an offer as appointment as a bishop. It means, literally, "I do not wish to be bishoped.") If the great paradox of Christianity means anything, it means this—that we must take the crown in our hands, and go hunting in dry places and dark corners of the earth until we find the one man who feels himself unfit to wear it. Culture was quite wrong; we have not got to crown the exceptional man who knows he can rule. Rather we must crown the much more exceptional man who knows he can't.*[28]

In the Sermon on the Mount, Jesus said, "Blessed are the meek, for they will inherit the earth" (Matthew 5:5, NIV). The meek inherit the Earth because they are the only ones that can be trusted

---
28 G. K. Chesterton, *Orthodoxy* (Musaicum Publishing, 2018).

with it. It is for those not full of themselves. It is for those that can be filled by God. To be humble is to be moldable and pliable—like clay on a potter's wheel. Stones have already made up their mind about what they are and what they are not. They are unyielding except for the painful process of chipping and chiseling away at them. That's painful for the stone and for the tool! But to be humble is not to be soft, at least not in the sense of being unsure of oneself or a pushover. Just because something's pliable doesn't mean it's fragile. Humility is a godly dependence and confidence.

> **False humility is another type of pride.**

You need to also be mindful of the trap of false humility. False humility is another type of pride. As I mentioned in chapter 1, in cultures like New Zealand, where people are likely to be chopped down if they stand out and up, it's called tall poppy syndrome—the tall poppies get cut down. Because of this, there can be a propensity to cut oneself down before anyone else has the chance to. False humility wants to appear humble, so it's paradoxically self-effacing with a self-promoting motivation.

Alternatively, false humility still holds one's opinions regarding oneself higher than God's, but their opinion is low. They then believe they are worth nothing and are crippled by fear and intimidation. Pride and false humility elevate our perspective of self above God's. God wants His opinions about us and about what's possible to shape our perspective.

Joshua is a great example of someone filled with the type of confidence God desires—a confidence that can only come from humility—a godly confidence. Joshua was told three times to be strong and courageous as he led the nation of Israel into the Promised Land (see Joshua 1). He wasn't told this because he could do it, and he had what it would take on his own. He was told to be strong and courageous because God had chosen him, God would be with him, and as Joshua lived according to God's words, he would live within a paradigm of protection and favor. Here are three observations on humility:

Humility Is an Invitation to Be Elevated

Because God exalts and gives grace to the humble, we invite God to elevate, promote, and expand us in all of the best possible ways. People often try to take what they believe is theirs, climb the ladders of power, and push their influence onto others. Leading in God's kingdom shouldn't be like this; if we're going to lead *for* Jesus, we have to lead *like* Jesus. We don't have to jostle for position, attempt to be noticed, or play power games to get ahead. When we pursue the path of humility—the path of the learner—we can trust that God will put us exactly where we need to be at the right time.

> If we're going to lead for Jesus, we have to lead like Jesus.

Humility Is a Virtue to Be Practiced

We can practice humility by seeking advice, asking lots of questions, being curious, following instructions from those more experienced, getting a mentor, and having people in our lives that can say no to us and whose correction and boundaries we heed. Every time we pray is also an expression of humility. The lack of a prayer life is really nothing other than pride. We think we can do it without God. When we apologize, repent, and seek forgiveness, we practice humility by admitting we are fallible and get it wrong. It doesn't make us weak; it makes us safe.

Growing up, I sometimes heard, "You can learn the easy way or the hard way." In other words, "Listen and do what I say or suffer the consequences." Perhaps you heard similar as a kid. I've come to believe that when it comes to learning life lessons, you can either learn from the mistakes of others or from your own. The former is hard. The latter is harder. While making our own mistakes is inevitable, many of them are avoidable. Humble leaders ask for advice—they defer to greater wisdom, knowledge, and experience. In all honesty, I have wondered how much pain I could have saved myself and those I lead if I'd been humble enough to ask for advice and follow it.

The extent of our humility can be measured by how well we receive feedback. When the feedback is encouragement, do we receive it or discount it? When the feedback is correction, can we receive it without the need to defend, excuse, or explain?

Humility Is Following in the Footsteps of our Rabbi, Jesus

We must have the same attitude as Christ and understand that as both Son of God and Son of Man, Jesus also had to grow. The apostle Paul described it this way:

> Though he was God, he did not think of equality with God as something to cling to. Instead, he gave up his divine privileges; he took the humble position of a slave and was born as a human being. When he appeared in human form, he humbled himself in obedience to God and died a criminal's death on a cross. Therefore, God elevated him to the place of highest honor and gave him the name above all other names, that at the name of Jesus every knee should bow, in heaven and on earth and under the earth, and every tongue declare that Jesus Christ is Lord, to the glory of God the Father. —**Philippians 2:6-11 (NLT)**

> Jesus grew in wisdom and stature and in favor with God and all the people. —**Luke 2:52 (NLT)**

Jesus's disciples were trained in His ways; they were apprenticed. They saw Jesus as their rabbi. The purpose of one's tutelage under a rabbi was to learn to view God, the Torah, the world, people, and issues the way they do. Like an aspiring carpenter learning their trade from an experienced one, the very nature of being a Christian is to be a learner. In a culture in which the term "Christian" is often used to describe someone other than a disciple, perhaps we have lost the importance of this idea, making the term relatively meaningless.

The term Christian (*Χριστιανός*) is only used three times in the New Testament to describe those who were believers. The term "disciple" (μαθητής meaning apprentice) is used 263 times. In fact, there are many people who would consider themselves Christians and hold orthodox beliefs according to the creeds but are not engaged in God's church and are not being transformed into Christlikeness. They might have the right beliefs but not transformed hearts and deeds.

I don't write this to judge, only to reveal that we need to redeem the idea of why people were originally called Christians in the first century. It wasn't because of the beliefs that they supposedly held but how those beliefs shaped the way they lived. Their lives resembled the life of Jesus Christ; therefore, they were called Christians, meaning "little Christs." It was a name given by others who observed a way of life, not a badge claimed by the individual because of their beliefs.

As leaders, we must rediscover the heart of what it means to be a Christian. That is, of course, to be the following:
- A disciple.
- An apprentice of the way of Jesus.
- A learner of a specific way of thinking and living.

We must learn to view our heavenly Father the same way Jesus does—to view and treat people as He demonstrates in Scripture, embracing how to engage with the world, how to commune, how to hope, and how to serve as He did, does, and would. As we rediscover this way of discipleship, we can inevitably model it and train others in it.

To Lead is Good.
To Lead is to Be an Example.
To Lead is to Pray.

> To Lead is to Grow in the Word.
> To Lead is to Trust.
> To Lead is to Learn.

Put This Into Practice

Reflect and journal on the following questions:

1. Whom do you need to go to in order to seek forgiveness as you repent?
2. Whom do you need to catch up with regularly to seek advice?
3. What do you need to be reading?
4. When was the last time you invited feedback?

PART II
leading others

chapter 7

to lead is to own it

"The Christian ideal has not been tried and found wanting. It has been found difficult; and left untried."
—G. K. Chesterton[29]

Have you ever seen a sports game where there is a ball to catch? When there are multiple players in the potential catching zone, someone always calls out, "Mine!" They are taking responsibility for ensuring the ball is caught, and they want to let their teammates know they don't need to worry because they have got it. They are catching it—they are owning it. Leadership isn't about running around yelling, "Yours!" It's about understanding

---

[29] G. K. Chesterton, *Chesterton Classics Collection: Orthodoxy, Heretics, What's Wrong With The World, What I Saw In America* (Independently Published, 2022) 203.

and owning what's mine—not in a selfish way, but in a way that brings clarity and, therefore, flow.

You can't lead what's in somebody else's hands. That's being a backseat driver, and we don't need any more of those in our churches and faith-based organizations. You have to feel the weight of it and take it upon your own shoulders to truly be a leader of it. If it's not your responsibility, you are not really the leader. That's why to lead is to own it.

Let's return to our earlier definition of leadership: to lead is to take responsibility for a desired future and to influence others to help create it.

There it is: to lead is to take responsibility.

> There it is: to lead is to take responsibility.

Responsibility Is a Pathway to Growth and Life

I still remember my dad teaching me how to swim. My grandparents had a swimming pool, and on hot summer days, we would visit them, so my parents could swim and cool off. One day, it was my time to learn, so my dad picked me up and threw me in. My grandad was in the pool, ready to help if needed. Help was needed. This was old-school swimming teaching. It was traumatic and probably gave a few people a fear of the water, but it worked for me. After a few times of being thrown in beyond where I could stand, I learned to tread water, stay afloat, and eventually, swim.

You see, the deep end is where you grow.

If you want to grow, you need to be stretched, and there are only two ways I know that will stretch you. One is a crisis. The second is being thrown into the deep end. Taking responsibility is a lot like jumping into the deep end. It can be scary, but it's part of how God wants to grow us and teach us to grow close to Him. In the deep end, we reach out for help. In the deep end, we discover we can do things we didn't know we could do. In the deep end, we realize there is more inside us than we give ourselves credit for, and it has a chance to come out.

From getting married at an early age and having an instant family to taking on events and responsibilities at church to becoming a senior pastor at age twenty-five, I've lived a life of either being thrown into the deep end or willingly jumping into it. I think I know a thing or two about the deep end!

While there have certainly been plenty of challenges in the deep end, I wouldn't trade it for anything. The blessings, growth, and impact far outweigh the battles. I wish more people would embrace responsibility earlier in their lives and in their churches because the sooner they do, the sooner they will grow.

Hired Hands vs. Shepherds

Jesus gives us the foundational concept of leading like Him; we must have an ownership heart and mindset towards the people we lead. We must be shepherds, not hired hands. Jesus said:

> I am the good shepherd. The good shepherd sacrifices his life for the sheep. A hired hand will run when he sees a wolf coming. He will abandon the sheep because they don't belong to him and he isn't their shepherd. And so the wolf attacks them and scatters the flock. The hired hand runs away because he's working only for the money and doesn't really care about the sheep.
>
> I am the good shepherd; I know my own sheep, and they know me, just as my Father knows me and I know the Father. So I sacrifice my life for the sheep. —**John 10:11-15 (NLT)**

As leaders of small groups, teams, or new Christians, we don't want to misunderstand this idea of ownership. Let's place the idea of owning it within its larger context. First and foremost, all people are God's people. They are not ours, and we can't let our ego or selfish ambition taint this idea of ownership. I'm a pastor, and I have been entrusted with a flock, which we call a church. My feelings mirror those of former Navy SEAL officers Jocko Willink and Leif Babin:

I dearly love the people God has entrusted to me.
I deeply care.
I intentionally take extreme ownership.[30]

I often wake up early or stay up late thinking about people, praying for people, and following up with people. I am passionate about ensuring people are connected, cared for, understood, helped, and growing. I spend endless hours preparing and delivering sermons to teach and equip people. I hurt when people leave, I grieve when people pass away, and I get angry when people

---
[30] Jocko Willink and Leif Babin, *Extreme Ownership: How U.S. Navy Seals Lead and Win* (New York, NY: St. Martin's Press, 2015).

attack the flock. I have given my entire adult life to the flock we lead. I own it. I take responsibility.

But they are not mine; they are God's. I am just an under-shepherd—an entrusted one. God sometimes moves people on to other shepherds. I get that. When that happens, my job is to bless them as they go. When I feel tempted to collect and hoard, I must remember that we are called to send and release. When I become insecure and jealous (probably just me, right?) that people are following this leader or listening to that pastor, I need to remember that my job is to own it, but I don't own them. Each person belongs to God!

> **When I become insecure and jealous (probably just me, right?) that people are following this leader or listening to that pastor, I need to remember that my job is to own it, but I don't own them.**

If we, as leaders, get this wrong, we can find ourselves becoming manipulative, anxious, and controlling. It's a sure recipe for a self-fulfilling prophecy of people looking for a new shepherd.

Now that we have that sorted, what does it mean to own it in a healthy way? Well, we have to know *who* and *what* is entrusted to us. Volunteer leaders in churches and faith-based organizations are typically entrusted with groups, teams, or projects and discipling new Christians or caring for people during tough times. We need to know that whatever it is, *the fundamental thing we are entrusted with is people.* The group isn't about the meetings, the team isn't about the tasks, and the project isn't about the ideas.

It's all about the people. If to lead is to own it, then the main thing we own is the people. Now, before you panic, let me explain what I mean by this (definitely not cults and slave labor—relax).

As leaders, we call out, "Mine!" in relation to the people entrusted to us. We are saying that we will catch them, that they will find love and safety in our hands, and that to the best of our ability, we won't drop them. We are saying that we are not just hired hands, but we are shepherds who love these people as we love ourselves. We don't put tasks and policies before people, but we will use everything at our disposal to help these people experience God's love and spiritual growth.

You need to see your role as a "mini pastor." Pastoring is a gift, not a job. I don't write this to overwhelm you but to keep you focused on the point of leadership, which is to play a part in helping others grow in God. Isn't that the desired future for which we are taking responsibility? Being a mini pastor looks like this:

- Living by example.
- Helping people get and stay connected in loving and godly relationships.
- Fostering a culture in our group, team, or relationship in which God-centered conversations are the norm.
- Praying for others.
- Showing grace instead of judgment.
- Lovingly confronting ungodliness.

- Turning up for others even when it's inconvenient.
- Asking for extra help if we need it.

As a pastor, I want to know that the people I have in leadership positions are owning what is most precious, and that's the people. I want to be able to assume that if they belong to your group, team, ministry, or world, they are known, loved, encouraged, supported, and growing. They are not getting dropped or falling through the cracks.

Hired hands, however, don't take ownership. This is most evident in two types of circumstances:

When Trouble Comes Their Way

When there's conflict, when things are not going well, when it's messy, when there's doubt, and when there are problems, the hired hands run for the hills. But the example Jesus sets for us is one of commitment and loyalty:

> Never let loyalty and kindness leave you!
> Tie them around your neck as a reminder.
> Write them deep within your heart.
> Then you will find favor with both God and people,
> and you will earn a good reputation. —**Proverbs 3:3-4 (NLT)**

Leading like Jesus means owning it—through the good times and the bad. People go through seasons, and so do organizations and churches. We have been through our fair share of tough, uncertain, and misunderstood times. I'm so thankful for the people that have faithfully led through it all. They have stood by the people that they lead and the churches in which they lead. It's this type of longevity and unoffendableness we need more of in our times. (I know unoffendableness isn't a real word, but I like it.)

When the Need for Self-Sacrifice Comes Their Way

Jesus laid down His life for the sheep. He loves them so much that He was willing to die so that they may live. This gives us a great example of how to own it in leadership. We must be willing to be inconvenienced—to sacrifice and to go without—so that others may experience the love, care, and growth God desires for them.

The old saying "No pain, No gain" doesn't just apply to the gym. It's also true of leadership; leaders embrace the pain, so those they lead can experience the gain. It's like being the lead cyclist in a peloton or a goose flying at the front of the V. It takes more effort, but it's what leaders do, so others can experience the ease. The reality of leadership is that the higher you climb, the less wriggle room you have. Imagine a pyramid. When you're at the bottom, there's lots of width, but the higher you go, the less width there is. That's the way it works. When you sign up for leadership, the expectations that are placed on you are always higher than the expectations placed on those you are leading.

Leadership means going further than those you are leading. Owning it is about laying your life down for those sheep. Do you sacrifice for them?

Owning Diligence

The other thing we have to own is whatever task or goal was entrusted to us. As a volunteer group leader, it might be to raise up and train another volunteer leader. As a volunteer team leader, it may be to execute a function within the church, such as helping people park their cars upon arrival; within a faith-based organization, it may be organizing a fundraising event or community meal. As a volunteer pastoral care leader, it might be praying for people after a gathering or throughout the week. As a volunteer operations leader, it might be ensuring that everyone is welcomed to church on a Sunday as they walk into the building and that the doors are opened and closed at the right times.

Being a leader in any area is to also own the entrusted task—to ensure the execution of the task is done with diligence and love. When we own what's entrusted to us and fulfill our task as a team, it makes a huge difference. All the different functions of the body of Christ work together to make the body what it is. It frees up others when a leader knows what they have been entrusted with, calls out "Mine!" and follows through by finding a way and getting it done.

It's no easy feat leading in today's environment in which people seem to have no problem canceling at the last minute, turning up late, or being careless in their attention to their task. But part of owning it is developing a culture for our teams where people understand the why, the how, the what, and the where feedback is given and the bar is raised. We want to build a culture of high jump, not limbo. In limbo, no matter how far you lower the bar, the people still try to slip under it. In high jump, when you raise the bar, people attempt to get over it. We want a high jump culture.

I don't mean a striving, performance-oriented culture; that's not a good reflection of kingdom values. I mean a culture of love for Jesus and a gratitude for what He has done. We want to be Spirit-empowered to do the very best with what is entrusted to us. Understand that your leadership work is work you do unto your God. We must hold ourselves and those we lead to the highest standards of kingdom ethics.

> Understand that your leadership work is work you do unto your God.

We Carry the Weight—Jesus Carries the Burden

Taking responsibility means there's a price to pay, but we are not used to paying it in our secular culture. In fact, society often teaches us the exact opposite: shirk responsibility when possible.

However, in God's kingdom, there's a beautiful weight to responsibility. The call of Jesus is to embrace it because, through responsibility, you grow too. There is another realm of intimacy with God, growth in Him, the satisfaction of a life being lived with purpose, and bearing fruit in others' lives.

But take heart; even though there is a weight to responsibility, we are not left to carry it on our own. Jesus helps us carry the burden.

> Then Jesus said, "Come to me, all of you who are weary and carry heavy burdens, and I will give you rest. Take my yoke upon you. Let me teach you, because I am humble and gentle at heart, and you will find

rest for your souls. For my yoke is easy to bear, and the burden I give you is light." —**Matthew 11:28-30 (NLT)**

We can only bear fruit in our leadership when we are connected to the vine that is Jesus. When we own it with our ultimate trust in God, the burden becomes a joy. The glove fits. Leadership has a new ease and makes us strong in the process.

However, taking responsibility too far by overestimating your value is a recipe for disaster. Thinking that everything rests on your shoulders is a pathway to burnout! Trust me. I've experienced that and have had to walk out the painful journey and repent. We must learn to hold a healthy tension between two truths:

1. Our contributions make a significant difference.
2. God is in control, so it doesn't all depend on us.

The main example of ministry burnout in Scripture is from the life of the prophet Elijah. He went from hero to zero all in one day. One moment, he was full of faith publicly, and the next moment, he was running in fear privately. He was depressed, suicidal, and ready to give up. How did this powerful person of God find himself burnt out? We get a hint in Elijah's response when God asked him twice: "What are you doing here, Elijah?" (1 Kings 19:9 and 13, NLT) Both times, Elijah replied:

"I have zealously served the Lord God Almighty. But the people of Israel have broken their covenant with you, torn down your altars, and killed every one of your prophets. I am the only one left, and now they are trying to kill me, too." —**1 Kings 19:10 and 14 (NLT)**

Twice, God asked His question, and Elijah gave the exact same response both times. Elijah thought he was the only one left; he thought it all rested on him. Elijah had been owning it, but in the wrong way—and that led to burnout. He had been leading and doing ministry with this sense that it was all on him the whole time, and eventually, something had to give. Have you ever felt this way? You are not alone. After giving Elijah further instructions, God's staggering response revealed the reality of Elijah's situation: "Yet I will preserve 7,000 others in Israel who have never bowed down to Baal or kissed him!" (1 Kings 19:18, NLT)

I have been there myself. In fact, the season in which I am writing this book is a season in which I am still journeying through it. I have ended up feeling like Elijah—depressed and over it, unable to face another day. As I continue to journey through burnout, I'm discovering that I had been owning it a little too much. My *doing for* Jesus had exceeded my *being with* Jesus. I wasn't trusting God with His people and His church enough. As I learn a better way to own it, I'm experiencing newfound joy in leading.

I can own it completely but carry it lightly!

I can own it completely but carry it lightly!

God is in control. Full stop. They are God's people; He is the ultimate Good Shepherd. Our leadership matters and makes a difference, but it doesn't all rest on us—God is building His church!

You can own it, and it can be a joy.

> **To Lead is Good.**
> **To Lead is to Be an Example.**
> **To Lead is to Pray.**
> **To Lead is to Grow in the Word.**
> **To Lead is to Trust.**
> **To Lead is to Learn.**
> **To Lead is to Own It.**

Put This Into Practice

1. Who has been entrusted to you? Write down their names. These are the precious people that God has brought into your life for you to disciple and care for.
2. What are all the tasks that have been entrusted to you? Write them down. What does truly owning these tasks look like?
3. Pray this prayer:

   Heavenly Father, I come to You weary,
   weighed down, and fatigued.
   I'm not sure if I can keep going.
   I thought that if I gave myself to Your
   work, I would feel fulfilled.
   Meet me in my emptiness; meet me in my fear.
   Minister to me in my fatigue; speak to me in my stress.
   You are the Good Shepherd; help me lie down
   and drink from your still waters.

Restore my soul.
Restore my mind.
Restore my emotions.
Restore my body.
Restore my relationships.
Restore me.
Forgive me, Lord, for my lack of trust, and grant me faith.
Good Shepherd, lead me, be with me, guide me,
sit with me, and pour Your oil all over me.
As I go from this time of prayer, may I go feeling lighter,
with Your peace and presence, with Your joy and love.
May I go and bring You glory.
Amen.

chapter 8
to lead is to care

"Make love be the measure of maturity."
—Pete Scazzero[31]

One of the greatest dangers for the modern church, with all its activity, is people feeling uncared for. If we are not careful, people can think that they don't matter. Have you ever felt that way? Many people already have deep insecurity or preloading to being sensitive to environments in which they sense they don't really matter. Sadly, if we are not intentional about caring for people in our churches and faith-based organizations, they can feel like another number, another task, another job, or another notch on the

---

31 Peter Scazzero, *Emotionally Healthy Discipleship: Moving from Shallow Christianity to Deep Transformation* (Grand Rapids, MI: Zondervan, 2021) 143.

belt. People can start to think, *I only matter if I produce, am involved, stay uncomplicated, and say yes to everything.* That cannot be!

> ## People must come first—before policy, before task, and before everything.

People matter most; they matter to God, and they must matter to us. People must come first—before policy, before task, and before everything. One of the ways we honor God is by caring for the people He has entrusted to us. That's why you matter as a leader so much. As you grow, step up, and embrace your mandate to lead, more people are able to be cared for. People are never a means to an end; they *are* the end. Use your team or tasks as opportunities to grow the people—not your people as an opportunity to produce another outcome.

The word "leadership" doesn't appear too often in the New Testament. While we can see people leading, and we see many concepts of leadership on display, the Bible often uses a different word to talk about those in church leadership. The word is best translated as shepherd. It's common today in our type of church to call leaders "pastors" (even though I don't encourage people to call me Pastor Joel; in fact, I actively discourage it).

Language Has a Vibe

Elder, overseer, deacon, shepherd, pastor, teacher—terminology can intimidate people. The language we use has a vibe. Language is loaded and comes with connotations, reactions, and feelings that might have nothing to do with the actual meaning or intended use of the word. I sometimes wonder if that's why many people don't see themselves as leaders. It's not because they lack the ability or desire to lead, but what that word has come to mean for them has been distorted. We can easily think of the A-type personality, the highly self-assured, and the outspoken, the preacher, or the CEO type. That's why we need to explain the Biblical terms and their contexts.

Peter, who became what we could call the leader of the Jewish church in the early part of Acts, was given a way to think about his commissioned leadership role. Before his denial, Jesus prayed for him and said,

> "Simon, Simon, behold, Satan demanded to have you, that he might sift you like wheat, but I have prayed for you that your faith may not fail. And when you have turned again, strengthen your brothers."
> —Luke 22:31-32 (ESV)

Before Jesus ascended, He had a powerful interaction with Peter around a fire, where He restored him from his denial and reaffirmed his calling. Jesus's instructions to him in John 21 (ESV) were "Feed my lambs" (verse 15), "Tend my sheep" (verse 16), and "Feed my sheep" (verse 17).

We can see and hear the tenderness in the leadership task Peter was being given. Jesus was shaping the paradigms and connotations of what it would mean for Peter to lead. Strengthen, tend, and feed. The shepherding language is impossible to miss. What Jesus had in mind when He called Peter to lead is the same thing

He has in mind when He calls us to lead—to care. Shepherds smell like sheep. They live with their sheep, are close to their sheep, and know their sheep by name. Our ability to lead well comes from our ability to care deeply.

> ## Our ability to lead well comes from our ability to care deeply.

Ancient shepherds cared, and modern-day leaders are called to care too.

God Wants His People to Flourish

God cares for us. Psalm 23 is one of the most beautiful pieces of literature on the planet (in my humble opinion). Its poetic brilliance shapes our imagination about our God who cares deeply for us. Living in God's care means that He is our Shepherd. We can be so secure and satisfied in our relationship with our Shepherd that we can honestly say, "If I have Him, I have everything I could ever need." He leads us to rest and restoration. He guides us on the right paths. He is with us through even the darkest times, protecting and guiding us even there. He prepares a table of delicious food and invites us to eat deeply with Him amid life's troubles and attacks. We are chosen and can live in overflow with the confidence that goodness and mercy will always be with us, and we will always be with our God.

We care because God first cared for us. That's biblical leadership!

For some of you, these words are a great encouragement. To others, they are a great challenge. To some, caring comes easily and naturally. To others, caring is an intentional daily (hourly!) decision. To lead like Jesus is to love others like Jesus did, and one-way love presents itself is in the form of care.

If you truly care, God can trust you to lead.

People flourish in environments where they are cared for. If you see someone doing really well, it will be because they are in an environment of care. Children flourish when cared for, and adults do too. A plant in the garden that's beautiful and bearing fruit is always the result of care: planting, pruning, tending, feeding, and watering. The more precious the plant, the more care required. Vegetable gardens or rose gardens don't just happen by accident; they require care. Likewise, the people we lead in our groups and teams must be cared for also.

So, if to lead is to care, how do we care, and what should we care about? While caring for people is more intuition than science, I believe, from my own pastoral experience, that there are eleven universal things we can all embrace:

Presence

Caring is about being present—turning up and incarnating. It's a tangible expression of God's love to another. When people are going through tough times, simply turning up and being present speaks volumes. Often, we can struggle to be present with others in their time of pain because we haven't learned to be present with our own pain and suffering. We have ignored it, skimmed over the surface, and not allowed ourselves to feel it. Once we can learn to be present in our own pain, we will experience a growing sense of comfort when being present with others.

Time

Time is our most precious resource that we can give people. Taking time to catch up, send a text, make a call, have coffee, help someone move house, or have a meal goes a long way to letting people know that you care. Enough cannot be said about having one-on-one time with people. We need to take intentional time to care for and ask plenty of questions of those we lead.

Listening

People find it hard to tell the difference between listening and love. We listen well when we listen to understand, not to reply. We can reflect back to the person what we hear them saying to check if we are understanding them correctly. Then, we can ask follow-up questions and go deeper.

Patience

Every parent knows that care requires patience. People, like sheep, can be messy. They don't walk in straight lines towards their destiny. They run all around the playground and sometimes, away from it! Caring requires giving people time and space to grow and develop; nobody feels cared for when they are being rushed.

Prayer

Prayer has already been covered extensively in an earlier chapter, but taking time to pray with people is a powerful expression of care. Entering God's presence together changes things and fosters intimacy.

Their Soul

Our soul is the sum of our inner world: our will, thoughts, and heart. The Bible teaches us to guard it as it's the wellspring of life (see Proverbs 4:23). Psalm 23:1-3 poetically proclaims that the Lord is our Shepherd and restores our souls. Jeremiah declared that if we walk the ancient paths, we will recover our souls (see Jeremiah 6:16). Jesus says that when we come to Him, walk with Him, and work with Him, we find rest for our souls (see Matthew 11:29). Peter, when writing to the church, said that we were once "straying like sheep, but have now returned to the "Shepherd and Overseer of your souls" (1 Peter 2:25, ESV). John wrote, "Beloved, I pray that all may go well with you and that you may be in good health, as it goes well with your soul" (3 John 1:2, ESV).

When we say that we care about a person's soul, we mean that we want to know how someone's inner world is going. How's their relationship with God? How are their spiritual practices? What's God been revealing, saying, and doing in their life? How's their emotional health? How's their thought life? Soul conversations are the conversations that matter the most. That's one of the reasons that the name of the church, which my wife and I lead, is Curate. Curate means to care for the soul.

> **Soul conversations are the conversations that matter the most.**

Relationships

The most satisfying area or the most devastating area of our lives is our relationships. It's where we can experience the greatest joys or suffer the greatest hurts. We all have a relational world. It might be in singleness, marriage, parenting, work, house-sharing, family, friends, dating, divorce, or engagement. We want to know how people are doing in their relational world. How are they living out discipleship in this area? What are their struggles, joys, and needs? Can we guide them towards extra help, such as professional counseling or mentoring?

Sustainability of Life Choices

Modern life is hard. Our problems might feel like First World problems, but that doesn't stop them from being problems. Many people live lives that are too busy, too full, and highly unsustainable—from the pressure of being constantly connected to chronic comparison. From the pursuit of lifestyle and recreation to the drive for success and financial pressure, life has a lot for us to juggle, right? Add to that the hours spent bingeing on Netflix, YouTube, and Instagram and the trajectory of people sleeping less and less.

No wonder burnout, depression, and anxiety are the illnesses of our time.

Now, add church to the mix and people's genuine desires to serve despite feeling they have to pretend that they have it all together. So, they keep on going and never remove the mask. They're fine, their life is fine, everything's fine. But it's really not.

That's a recipe for disaster.

Many people get passionately involved in church, only to run out of steam and burn out further down the road. Sadly, as the body of Christ, we have often looked the other way when people are living life at an unsustainable pace, happy to take the good while it's being given. Caring for the individual, however, means not repeating this pattern. We need to help people order their lives around what matters most.

At one extreme, there are people who are unable to commit to doing anything in church because they are "so busy." Yet the reality is that they use their time poorly, spending twenty hours a week on their phone and staying up too late hanging out with their friends. "Too busy" is often code for a life not ordered according to God's priorities. At the other extreme, we need to be the voice of moderation to the people who are too involved or do not have enough balance, given the season of their life.

I'd rather see someone involved in serving the Lord through their local church for their whole life at a lesser level than someone who gives a lot of hours for only a brief season because they burn out from it. To care is to ask the tough questions—to care more about them than what they can do for you—and slow down long enough to hear their answers.

> **To care is to ask the tough questions and slow down long enough to hear their answers.**

Attitudes

Attitudes shape our dispositions, and dispositions become our character. To care for the people that we lead is to begin recognizing which attitudes align with godly character and which ones do not. There are attitudes in our culture and churches that have become acceptable yet are not aligned with God's Word revealed in Scripture—attitudes of unforgiveness, dishonor, gossip, and slander. People choose to harbor offenses rather than sailing their ship to the person with whom they have an issue, talking it out, forgiving, and moving on.

We care when we encourage godly attitudes and challenge ungodly ones.

We often don't have to come in with a full-frontal attack, and generally, people don't respond well to that anyway. Asking people why they think a certain way, what they think God thinks about their attitude, what the Bible says about that, and where that hurt comes from can help lead people towards freedom.

Encouragement

I often have people give me a compliment or encouragement and follow it up with, "But don't get a big head!" This is the Kiwi way (New Zealander way) of chopping people back down because we have believed the lie that encouragement can lead to pride. Here's the thing: in all my years of leadership, I have never seen anyone become full of pride because of too much encouragement. However, I have seen others not become everything they could because of a lack of it.

Most people are starving for encouragement, and I don't think you can ever encourage someone enough. What gets celebrated gets repeated. When we encourage, we are not only caring for people's inner worlds by blowing fresh wind into their being, but we are also spurring them on to greater godliness. Encouragement gives people fresh life, fresh passion, and fresh resolve. It helps them put their shoulders back and lift their head high. When you receive encouragement from your leader, you always feel cared for, so encourage the people you lead as much as you can. Send them a text, start a meeting by celebrating some people, and speak words of life into them.

Remember: the power of life and death is in the tongue (see Proverbs 18:21).

Genuine Interest

If what matters to them matters to you, people will feel cared for. Being interested in their family, work, business, hobbies, and aspirations goes a long way. Remembering birthdays, anniversaries, and hard days because of death and grief, wiring a card, making a phone call, or sending a text means a lot to people when dealing with those moments in their lives. Knowing someone had a job interview, praying for them, and checking in with how it went are huge expressions of care.

> ## Care for people by being on the journey with them.

Care for people by being on the journey with them.

To Lead is Good.
To Lead is to Be an Example.
To Lead is to Pray.
To Lead is to Grow in the Word.
To Lead is to Trust.
To Lead is to Learn.
To Lead is to Own It.
To Lead is to Care.

Put This Into Practice

I quoted Peter Scazzero, author of *Emotionally Healthy Discipleship: Moving from Shallow Christianity to Deep Transformation*, at the beginning of this chapter. He has formulated some helpful questions you can ask next time you are catching up with someone in your care.[32]

1. How are your rhythms and time with Jesus?
2. How is your marriage or singleness going?
3. Tell me about your top 1-3 priorities/goals and the challenges you are facing.
4. What is your next step for your development and growth—both personally and in your ministry?
5. What one thing can I be praying with you about?

---

32 Peter Scazzero, *Emotionally Healthy Discipleship: Moving from Shallow Christianity to Deep Transformation*.

chapter 9

to lead is
to serve

"If serving is beneath you, leading is beyond you."
—Author Unknown

Many of our modern-day examples of leadership come with images of being served: royalty, politicians, CEOs, and, sadly, sometimes, pastors. Holding positions of influence can make leaders assume that they have people to do things for them—right now. We have all watched shows where the leader has assistants to take care of every need or whim, and everyone else in the organization exists to make their life easier. But that's not the way of Jesus. Nor is it the way He taught us to lead.

People want to be led by people who are servants, not kings and queens.

Jesus said that whoever wants to be the greatest must be a servant (see Matthew 20:26, NLT). The way of leading in the church isn't so much a journey upwards as it is downwards. It's not a race to the top but a race to the bottom. It's easy to think about leading as being able to make the decisions, call the shots, and get others to do what you want, but that is not Jesus-style leadership. To lead, according to Jesus, is to serve.

> To lead, according to Jesus, is to serve.

Embracing Leading As Serving

You are, perhaps, familiar with the story of Jesus on the night before He gave up His life on the cross. It's recorded for us in John 13. He was about to have a meal with His disciples. Jesus took off His robe, put on a towel, and began to wash His disciples" feet. When He had finished, He said,

> "If I then, your Lord and Teacher, have washed your feet, you also ought to wash one another's feet. For I have given you an example, that you also should do just as I have done for you. Truly, truly, I say to you, a servant is not greater than his master, nor a messenger greater than the one who sent him." —John 13:14-16 (ESV)

How was the Son of God able to serve His disciples in this way? A clue is given to us just before the feet washing takes place: "Jesus knew that the Father had given him authority over everything and that he had come from God and would return to God" (John 13:3, NLT).

Jesus knew who He was, where He had come from, and where He was going. We will not be truly free to serve until we know who we are, where we have come from, and where we are going. If we do not know these things like Jesus did and aren't grounded in them, we may do things that *look like* serving, but they will not be with a *servant's heart*. They will just be another means to self-gain.

Jesus Knew Who He Was

Jesus had a perspective that created in Him an internal security. This internal security allowed Him to embrace serving, knowing His identity wasn't wrapped up in His function. When our sense of security or self is wrapped up in anything less than God, we find ourselves needing to find it through external means: status, wealth, or being treated as important. If that's the case, we are never truly free to serve.

The ability to serve comes from knowing who you are in your Heavenly Father through Christ Jesus. In the same way Jesus knew all authority had been given to Him, we can know what's been given to us as followers of Jesus. We have been adopted and made children of God. We are a part of His royal priesthood by His grace and through our faith. Like the younger son returning home in the story of the prodigal son, the father put a ring on his finger, a robe on his back, and sandals on his feet. These were symbols of his being restored to his former status in the family. We, too, have been given sonship and daughtership with our Heavenly Father through Jesus.

Jesus Knew Where He Came From

We become free to serve when we stay grounded in our story. While Jesus came from Heaven, we did not. We came from the Earth. We do well to remind ourselves that, but by the grace and mercy of God, we would not be here. It's His breath in our lungs, it's His sacrifice that grants forgiveness, and it's His grace making us whole. God doesn't owe you *anything*, but in Jesus, He has already given you *everything*.

> God doesn't owe you anything, but in Jesus, He has already given you everything.

Jesus Knew Where He Was Going

After His death, resurrection, and ascension, Jesus knew He would return to His Father. We are assured of the same promise. Jesus has gone to prepare a place for us. Isn't that wonderful? It's a living hope of an inheritance in eternity that does not decay and is secure. This hope is an anchor for our souls, allowing us to live securely in the *here and now*, knowing that the *then* is set in stone.

Once we are grounded in who we are, where we have come from, and where we are going according to God, we become free to serve. But how do we actually live this out in our own lives? There are three things that Jesus did in the following verse, which we can apply to our own lives of leadership today:

> So he got up from the table, took off his robe, wrapped a towel around his waist, and poured water into a basin. Then he began to wash the disciples' feet, drying them with the towel he had around him.
> —John 13:4-5 (NLT)

Jesus got up. We have to get up. I'm not being metaphorical. I'm being literal—plain and simple. Get up in the morning, get out there, and turn up to serve! So much of serving is just getting yourself out of bed and showing up to the people and places that need you. We have to get out of our selfishness, out of our comfort, and out of our convenience if we are to serve. Get out of consumerism, individualism, and entitlement.

Jesus was reclining at the table, enjoying Himself. I bet He was comfortable. But He got up. The reality was that someone needed to wash everyone's feet; it was the accepted and common practice. Normally, the lowliest servant in rank would do the job. Perhaps the disciples were wondering who would do it. Perhaps they were impatiently waiting for someone to do it, so they could eat but saw the task as beneath themselves. What do you need to get up out of in order to embrace serving the people you lead?

Jesus took off. He took off His robe. Jesus's robe was flash for His time. It was valuable—a garment that fitted His status as a rabbi. It was so valuable that it was gambled for after His death rather than torn and divided (see Matthew 27:35). His robe would have identified Him to others; it said something about who He was, like a police uniform helps us identify a police officer, or a designer outfit alludes to someone's possible earnings. So, when Jesus took off His robe, it was more than just about being appropriately dressed for the task of washing feet. He was intentionally taking off His external status symbol as a rabbi.

You have robes that you have collected throughout your life thus far: business owner, successful lawyer, or former sports star and wealth, houses, cars, clothes, or experiences. Robes are the external symbols of status. They are how we want others to perceive us. To be a servant, we must learn to take those robes off.

Jesus put on. He put on a towel. He exchanged His robe for a towel. He took off His suit and put on a high-visibility vest. He pulled up in His brand-new luxury car after making deals all day and put on rubber gloves, grabbing a bucket ready to clean some toilets.

Jesus embraces a great reversal.

Washing someone's feet wasn't just a customary gesture of hospitality in Jesus's culture. It was a lowly task. If you didn't have a servant, the wife would wash the husband's feet. If you had children, the youngest child would do it, and if you had many servants, the lowest-ranked one would be tasked with it. In other words, Jesus embraced the lowliest of servant tasks when He chose to put on the towel.

If we are to serve like Jesus, we need to learn to take off and put on. We need to take off our entitlement and put on gratitude. Take off our rights and put on our responsibilities. Take off our idea that we are so important and so busy and put on the humility to sit with the people we lead. I am inspired by the many people in our church who are examples of this very thing. Amazing business people are found cleaning toilets at church on a Sunday, wealthy individuals set up for the church children's program, and sports stars spend their weekends mentoring teenagers. Mums and dads, who have been juggling their own families all week, take time to teach and care for other people's children on a Sunday. Young adults in the midst of their own education and part-time jobs gather in prayer meetings for others.

God has given us a figurative robe through His Son, Jesus. We have been made sons and daughters of the Most High. But He invites us into a way of leading that doesn't cling to robes. We can practice this way of servanthood in all aspects of our life. We can serve our spouse, our family, and our friends. We can serve our colleagues, our boss, or our employees. We can serve our church, our fellow brothers and sisters, and our neighbors.

And in all of it, we are serving God.

A Concern for Their Whole Life

We can serve the people we lead by helping them figure out how to follow Christ well in their everyday lives. After all, the church's primary area of ministry is the daily life of its members, not the Sunday gathering. Most Christians spend most of their life working, eating, relating, sleeping, and going about their lives. We spend very little of our time gathered for corporate worship, prayer, the Lord's Supper, and growing in the Word.

> **The church's primary area of ministry is the daily life of its members, not the Sunday gathering.**

As leaders, we want to serve those we lead by providing help and support to them, integrating their faith in all areas of their lives. Fostering spiritual practices, learning to see their work as a holy vocation, and teaching them to raise their families in the ways of the Lord. Supporting them to live out their singleness or marriage as the Lord would have them do so. We don't just want people feeling connected to God through organized church activity. We don't just want people feeling a sense of purpose when they are serving in our organizations. We want people to know God in all of their lives and live their whole lives with a sense of purpose. That requires service.

Laying aside our agendas, slowing down, and asking some thoughtful questions make a huge difference. We can assume a lot, and a lot can go unnoticed. Ask about their lives, and support them with their questions, doubts, struggles, and practices. At first, it will feel like you have waded into a mess, but rather than being swept under the rug, the mess is better out in the open where God's grace is able to flow through it. If we can help people live well in all areas of life, not only will they flourish, but whatever it is we are leading will also flourish. They will bring their health to the team and serve more sustainably and with longevity.

To Lead is Good.
To Lead is to Be an Example.
To Lead is to Pray.
To Lead is to Grow in the Word.
To Lead is to Trust.
To Lead is to Learn.
To Lead is to Own It.

To Lead is to Care.
To Lead is to Serve.

Put This Into Practice
1. Reflect upon and journal about these questions:
   - What do you need to take off or put on?
   - How can you serve the people you are leading?
   - How can you be an example of a servant to them?
   - How could you motivate your small group or team to serve others in a greater way?
2. Now, make it personal: list the people in your realm of influence and write down one specific way you could serve each one of them.
3. In what areas of their lives could you help them flourish?

chapter 10
to lead is to recruit

Don't say someone's no for them.
—Joel Milgate

Jesus had a master plan. He came to Earth, lived many years in obscurity, being formed through the normal rhythms of life, and then, at age thirty, burst on the scene and began His public ministry. He knew His public ministry would lead to His crucifixion, resurrection, and then His ascension back to the Father. While this would be the end of His ministry on Earth, it would not be the end of His ministry. It was always His intention that His followers would continue His mission to proclaim the good news and make disciples throughout the earth.

> **It was always Jesus's intention that His followers would continue His mission to proclaim the good news and make disciples throughout the earth.**

The only problem was that when He started, He didn't have any followers or disciples. Isn't that comforting? We can take encouragement from Jesus and the fact that that's how everyone starts on their leadership journey. It may even be many people's biggest fear when it comes to leadership, with thoughts like *If I step up to lead, will anyone follow?*

That's how most of us start when we step up into leadership. We are given a group or a team to lead; the only problem is that there isn't a group or a team yet (unless you have been transitioned to lead an already existing one). We have been commissioned and given a realm of authority and responsibility, but we don't have any people to lead yet. Like Jesus, we can have a vision to fulfill, but starting with a blank sheet of paper can be tough. After all, are you really a leader if you're not leading anyone? (Well, technically, you're not, but once you put this chapter into practice, you will have some people to lead!)

Go and Find Your People

Jesus didn't wait for His disciples to find Him; He went and found them. He went to where they were; He personally recruited them—face-to-face. He took the risk, and He opened up His life to them. He identified whom He wanted in His group and team. He took the responsibility to ensure they knew He wanted them to be a part of what He was doing. In addition, He recruited people that the religious system of His day would never have. He went to the smelly fishermen, the distrusted tax collector, and the passionate zealot—the people who wouldn't make it to a second interview for the school of the rabbis!

And yet, the power of His recruitment, the calling on their lives, the influence of His discipleship, and the empowerment of the Holy Spirit caused these twelve guys—as well as the many women and men who also followed Jesus—to turn the world upside down. And two thousand years later, we are doing what we are doing because they were first recruited.

When I consider some of the best leaders and team members in our church, almost all of them were recruited. They didn't initiate becoming a volunteer. They didn't come and ask to be involved—we identified them. Almost every single one of our staff has been recruited. Potential was seen in them, conversations were had, prayers were prayed, and the result was people stepping up and serving the Lord in greater ways. Some of your best future volunteers are waiting to be asked to get involved, so let's get ready to become recruiters and make the ask!

In the book of Numbers, Moses told God that he'd had enough of the burden of leadership sitting solely on him:

> "I can't carry all these people by myself! The load is far too heavy! If this is how you intend to treat me, just go ahead and kill me. Do me a favor and spare me this misery!" —**Numbers 11:14-15 (NLT)**

Read God's reply:

> "Gather before me seventy men who are recognized as elders and leaders of Israel. Bring them to the Tabernacle to stand there with you. I will come down and talk to you there. I will take some of the Spirit that is upon you, and I will put the Spirit upon them also. They will bear the burden of the people along with you, so you will not have to carry it alone." —Numbers 11:16-17 (NLT)

As a result, Moses got to work; he recruited and gathered people, inviting them to share the load (see Numbers 11:24). And God did what He said He would do: He put His Spirit on them to help them with the task so that it might be shared.

What's the lesson for us? If we do not recruit well, we will eventually get worn down and discouraged. Don't wait for people to volunteer but then complain that no one wants to help. Go and ask them—find your people!

> **Don't wait for people to volunteer but then complain that no one wants to help. Go and ask them—find your people!**

I want you to zoom out for a moment. Imagine with me the potential impact that your recruitment could make. The ripple effect of the people you recruit into your group or team could have untold effects. Their impacted lives could mean changes in their families, legacies, workmates, friends, and extended families. This wave of impact could keep rolling for generations.

All because you took the time to recruit.

There's a well-known saying of unknown origin: "If you want to go fast, go alone, but if you want to go far, go together." A lesson from polar expeditions through the ages teaches us that there are some journeys we shouldn't do alone. Many people have been lost on the ice doing it alone. It's the nature of sustainable leadership to never do it alone.

If we want to have people to lead—and one day people to replace us—we need to go find them and recruit them. The onus is on us.

How to Recruit Well

Have a Vision to Cast

Simon Sinek's book *Start with Why* reminds us of the power of a vision.[33] Vision inspires people; it moves people and excites them to get involved. People don't sacrifice for a *what*, but they will give their lives for a noble *why*. We see this in the most effective brands all around the world. They don't sell us on a product; they sell us on a why. People display brand loyalty when they buy into the why. People don't buy Apple products because they are necessarily superior. They buy into Apple's why, which is about thinking differently.

To put it simply:

---

[33] Simon Sinek, *Start with Why: How Great Leaders Inspire Everyone to Take Action* (London, ENG: Penguin Business, 2019).

- Vision is the why.
- Values are the how.
- Tasks are the what.

In the gospel of Matthew, Jesus cast a compelling vision that changed the course of Peter's life: "Come, follow me, and I will show you how to fish for people!" (Matthew 4:19, NLT)

Notice what Jesus did? He gave Peter a vision of who he could become. And Jesus made it clear that He was committed to helping Peter become that very person. Such a direct, personal, vision-filled invitation caused Peter to leave his business, his family, and his community. Such is the power of vision.

Think about vision on three levels when recruiting volunteers:

Level One: *The vision of the church or faith-based organization*

Call this the overarching vision. The big vision. We need to be able to articulate this, so there is only one vision. We want to know how our group or team is helping to fulfill the big vision. Division occurs when there are multiple visions. For example, the vision of the church that my wife and I lead is: "To be a people pursuing the way of Jesus and playing our part in His story."

Level Two: *The vision of the group, team, or project*

Your group, team, or project exists for a reason! Maybe it's a short-term group to grow in a certain area. Maybe it's a team that welcomes people each Sunday, ensuring everyone has a positive, personal, and friendly experience. Maybe it's a missions project, serving a local school or organization in some specific way. Whatever it is, your group, team, or project exists for a reason. It also has a why. Here are some examples from my own church:

Alpha Group: *"Our vision is to help people come to faith."*

Small Group: *"Our vision is to practice Jesus-centered community, so we might all become more like Christ."*

Welcoming Team: *"Our vision is to give people a good experience, so they become open to a God experience."*

Coffee Team: *"Our vision is to foster community through hospitality."*

Local Missions Team: *"Our vision is to live out the gospel, being the hands and feet of Jesus in our local community."*

All of the above group visions help fulfill the overarching vision.

Level Three: *The vision for the person you are recruiting*

We want to always have a sense of how we can help the person we are recruiting grow and fulfill God's calling over their life. As secular culture grows ever more individualistic, this matters more than ever. People want to know what's in it for them and how it's going to help them. Elaborating further on this is not part of the scope of this book, but it is important to understand it. As leaders, we can't just give lip service to this part of vision. We need to see our roles as leaders in their lives for the purpose of helping them grow, especially in Christ.

Know Your Nonnegotiables

The next step in recruitment is to be clear about the how and the what—the values and the task. All churches and faith-based organizations have values. Some are articulated; some are not. Curate Church has five core values: Love, Mission, Spiritual Practices, Togetherness, and Authenticity. These guide and shape our culture. When people come into contact with our community, they should feel the outworking of these values. People often comment about the passion our people have for God, the love our people have for each other, and the authenticity of the whole community. The further people step into involvement within our church, the more often these values get talked about and celebrated.

Why does this matter when it comes to recruitment? Because we want to be clear from the outset what we expect from people if they join our group or team. We don't want to trick people! We want to set clear expectations. Being clear about how your team or group will conduct themselves or how a project will be completed is paramount. If, for example, there are homework and preparation involved with expectations regarding timeliness and availability, it would be good for them to know, right? Be as clear as possible, but don't overwhelm them. It's not about the rules; it's about the guiding values. You don't need to create guiding values for your specific team; figure out what the existing overarching core values for your church or organization mean for your area!

Get Down to Business

Now that we have sorted out the why and the how, the next focus can be on the what—the task that you will actually be doing. For example, asking someone to attend your group each time it meets, asking someone to serve on your team every second week, or asking someone to join your project next month. The what is the stuff.

Remember this: how you recruit someone is how you have to keep them. If you compromise for their involvement, you will be forever compromising. Jesus let plenty of people walk away that wanted to follow Him on their own terms. As leaders, we need to do the same.

> Jesus let plenty of people walk away that wanted to follow Him on their own terms. As leaders, we need to do the same.

Set Up a Meaningful Conversation

The best way to recruit a volunteer is through an intentional and personal conversation. If it matters, it's worth doing properly. Don't just send out a few texts or post something online. Don't ask for help in a needy sense; cast a vision for what could be. Start by thinking about three to six people in your life that you think would be inspired by the vision and may want to be a part of what you are leading. Don't say people's no for them—they can say their own no if it's not for them. Don't sell yourself short by assuming they won't want to follow you, and don't poach people from other teams or groups!

Once you have a list of names, spend a few days praying for each one, and see what the Lord reveals. Ask God to prepare their hearts (and yours) for the conversation. Follow any prompts you may receive. It's then time to set up some appointments. Contact each one, and say you want to meet up with them to talk about something in which you would love to have them involved. Hopefully, they accept the invitation, and the time will come to meet up.

This is when volunteer leaders can get a bit nervous. *What exactly do I say? How do I word it?* Here's a practical example (a script, if you will) to give you some inspiration to find your own words:

Hey, you know how our church wants to see everyone in community? (Big vision)

Well, I have decided to step up and lead a group to help see this vision fulfilled. (Leading by example)

I'm excited to lead a group where anyone can belong, we do life together, and we help each other grow in our faith. (Group vision)

When I was thinking of and praying about this group, I thought of you. I think this group would be a great next step for you. I think you would grow and flourish in your own gifts and talents and grow spiritually. (Vision for the person)

We are going to live out the church values together and meet each fortnight on a Tuesday at 7 pm. We are going to give it a go for a year, and if you decide to be a part of it, I would like it to be a priority for you. We will take breaks during the school holidays. If, after coming a few times, it's not the right fit for you, that's okay! But if you do want to continue, I only ask that you would be committed to it and the people in it. (The how and the what)

I don't want your answer now. I want you to pray about it for a week and come back to me with any thoughts and questions you may have. I'll follow you up in a week if I don't hear from you. How does that sound?

After giving your recruitment pitch, answer any questions they may have, and give them time to share their thoughts, but don't press them for a commitment. To clarify, we don't always need to recruit like this, especially when it comes to groups. Often, we will just meet people who are not yet connected—but desire to be—during Sunday gatherings or in other environments; in these circumstances, a simple invitation is sufficient. However, catching up personally to clearly articulate the vision and expectations for the group never hurts—it only expresses more love and care to the person desiring to be connected!

The bigger the ask, the more intentional we need to be about how we recruit.

> **The bigger the ask, the more intentional we need to be about how we recruit.**

See What God Does

There's no need to manipulate, oversell, or pressure. You want people whom God is leading to be with you, and you don't want people whom God is not leading or who are reluctant. When you give people time to hear from God or make a decision away from the pressure, you empower them. Then you know that if they say yes, they are committed to it, and they own it. If they want to be a part of the honest vision you shared with them, they will join, and it will be entirely their decision. Later, down the road, you don't need to worry as much about the risk of resentment. After all, they weren't pressured or manipulated into anything. God knows what you need and whom you need; if you engage in an intentional process with space for God to work, you can trust His timing.

Be encouraged by the fact that the success rate of recruiting effectively is astonishingly high. Many people are not a part of your team and group, not because they don't want to be, but because they haven't been asked in a meaningful and inspiring way!

> To Lead is Good.
> To Lead is to Be an Example.
> To Lead is to Pray.
> To Lead is to Grow in the Word.
> To Lead is to Trust.
> To Lead is to Learn.
> To Lead is to Own It.
> To Lead is to Care.
> To Lead is to Serve.
> To Lead is to Recruit.

Put This Into Practice

The following table is something I use to keep track of the different people I have approached to join a team. A blank copy is provided in Appendix 3. Try it out! Or use it as inspiration to create a system that works for you.

People to Recruit:	Meeting Booked For:	Had the Meeting:	Follow Up On:	Outcome:
Joel Milgate	Saturday, 3 July	Yes	17 July	Keen to join

chapter 11

to lead is to develop

CFO: "What happens if we invest in developing our people, and then, they leave us?"
CEO: "What happens if we don't, and they stay?"

I wouldn't be who I am today without the people who have taken time to intentionally develop me—from youth leaders when I first started following Jesus to mentors and my pastor. What did all these people have in common? They took time to have intentional conversations with me and stretched me in my walk and work with God. They helped me understand the different seasons and stages of life, imparting wisdom to help me grow on my own.

> Teach us to realize the brevity of life, so that we may grow in wisdom.
> —Psalm 90:12 (NLT)

The real work begins once we have recruited people to join our team or group. Why? Because it's not about *collecting* people; it's about *developing* people. We want the environment around our leadership to be like a river: once you hop in, you're going to be taken somewhere new. This is an approach that is different from other leadership environments that could be likened more to a lake at best or a swamp at worst.

Lakes form where the water has nowhere to go; lakes collect as much as possible. Some churches can easily become more about gathering than sending. Swamps form when the water is shallow and the flow is too slow. Some churches can become like this, too, but I believe God wants His environments to be like rivers. We want our churches and organizations to be like rivers, taking people somewhere. For that to happen, those in leadership need to think about how they are going to develop the people they lead.

It's not about collecting people; it's about developing people.

Jesus led His disciples this way. He took these guys from being fishermen and misfits to becoming apostles and mighty Spirit-filled men of God who pioneered the early church. From the moment they were recruited, they hopped into a river of development. Simply collecting followers was not Jesus's main focus—developing them in order to send them out was. This must be the way we look at leading too.

Leaders can often be satisfied with collecting people—having enough on their team or in their group. We must remember why we signed up to lead in the first place: it's about the people—who they can become and what they can accomplish with God in His kingdom.

I keep in mind the following four goals I have for the people I am helping develop:

1. They would walk closer with God.
2. They would become more like Jesus.
3. They would be equipped for their current assignment.
4. They would become leaders themselves.

In other words, developing someone means discipling them. Let's unpack this.

Discipling Leaders

We Need the Mindset of Jesus

Jesus knew His ministry on Earth wouldn't last forever. I believe that this time pressure contributed to His impetus to develop His disciples, so they could continue the mission after His ascension. We need to see our leadership the same way. We need to lead with both an *ease* and an *urgency*. We don't want to be rushed or in a hurry, but we need a sense of urgency:

- People's souls are at stake.
- We don't know when Jesus is coming back.
- We don't know when we will be called upon to lead something or somewhere else.

When we lead with the mindset that we won't be around in the same way in a few years' time, it brings focus and fire to being a developer.

Jesus understood the big mission and vision of God the Father. Jesus wasn't leading to have a successful ministry just in His time. In fact, by all measures at His death, it would have been considered mostly unsuccessful! He was birthing what we now call *the church*. The body of Christ. And it would be His church that would go to the ends of the earth, even to this day, taking the good news to those that haven't heard it yet, at the same time learning to live in the kingdom and partner with God in making all things new everywhere. We have to keep our eyes on the vision and mission of God; He doesn't want any to perish but all to come to salvation (see 2 Peter 3:9). Every person developed is another person commissioned to participate in what God is doing.

We Must Develop People to Walk Closer With God

> Are you tired? Worn out? Burned out on religion? Come to me. Get away with me and you'll recover your life. I'll show you how to take a real rest. Walk with me and work with me—watch how I do it. Learn the unforced rhythms of grace. I won't lay anything heavy or ill-fitting on you. Keep company with me and you'll learn to live freely and lightly.
> —Matthew 11:28-30 (MSG)

Our entire life's potential comes from our relationship with God. Jesus said, "Abide in me, and I in you. As the branch cannot bear fruit by itself, unless it abides in the vine, neither can you, unless you abide in me" (John 15:4, ESV). Jesus invited us to first *come* to Him that we might learn to *walk* with Him. We want to help people develop their relationship with God, encouraging them in spiritual practices that will enrich their depth and experience of walking with God in their daily lives.

We Must Develop People to Become Like Jesus

Paul said, "Imitate me as I imitate Christ" (1 Corinthians 11:1, ESV). What a bold imperative! We develop people into Christlikeness by first being an example. That doesn't mean being perfect, but it does mean being intentional. We ensure that the conversations we are having with our team or group are conducive to helping people be strengthened in Jesus. It's clear in Paul's letter to the Philippians that there are a lot of things we can talk about, but not everything is fruitful. Keep people focused on that which is most profitable for building people up:

> Finally, brothers, whatever is true, whatever is honorable, whatever is just, whatever is pure, whatever is lovely, whatever is commendable, if there is any excellence, if there is anything worthy of praise, think about these things. What you have learned and received and heard and seen in me—practice these things, and the God of peace will be with you. —Philippians 4:8-9 (ESV)

We Must Develop People to be Equipped for Their Assignment

It may seem obvious, but it's surprising how many leaders miss this crucial part of development: take time to develop people, so they know what is expected of them in their team or group. Help them to know the answers to the following questions:

- What's our team's culture?
- What's our team's purpose?
- What's our approach to completing tasks?
- What's our expectation for each person in the group?

Don't assume these things; they need to be modeled, talked about, and expressly developed in the people we lead. Mission leaks, and vision drifts. What seems crystal clear one day can become as clear as mud the next. We must develop clarity on culture, vision, mission, and task in whatever it is we lead. When you think people are sick of hearing about this stuff, they may just be finally getting it!

> **We need to intentionally train people for their tasks, making sure they receive the skills, feedback, and upskilling they need to grow.**

We need to intentionally train people for their tasks, making sure they receive the skills, feedback, and upskilling they need to grow. People are motivated when they improve and take on bigger challenges. Good people want more feedback, not less. In addition, we must think of the other roles and related assignments people have in their lives—being a spouse, a parent, an employee or employer, a caregiver, or a student. We help people figure out how to live out these assignments through the lens of becoming like Jesus and doing what He would do if He were them. When this happens, people have a sense of living every day on purpose for and with God.

We Must Develop People to Become Leaders Themselves

As disciples of Jesus, God desires each of us to be developed, so we, too, can lead and make disciples of others. We want to lead everyone towards this goal. I've noticed two types of developers; both are equally valuable. Understanding these two types will help you figure out which one you are and how to go about developing others.

Pioneers—I'm a pioneer by nature. Pioneers like to start things. They break new ground and are entrepreneurial in nature. Thoughts of something new, starting from scratch, and doing something that's never been done before excites them. They typically get bored when stuck in the same position for too long or when they find themselves doing the same thing for a long period of time.

Pioneers don't like to be static! They usually develop others in order to transition out of something established and pioneer again. They start a group or team and develop the next leader to take it over, so they can start another group or team. They pioneer a project, get things started, and develop a leader to take it on, so they can get the next project off the ground. Pioneering developers are looking to replace themselves, so they can move on to new things. They multiply impact by raising people up and moving out of the way. The apostle Paul is an example of a pioneer. He went from city to city, establishing churches, raising people up, and moving on.

Settlers—Settlers like to stay put. I'm definitely not a settler, but I need settlers. They settle in and develop others to be sent out. In a group context, they may develop several new leaders over a few years and send them all out to establish new groups. A settler may lead the same group or team for years on end, but the impact from the people they have developed is anything but static. A settler multiplies impact by raising people up and sending them out. The apostle James is an example of a settler. He was the apostle in Jerusalem, and he developed and strengthened the church from this place.

> **A leader who fails to develop a successor fails.**

Identifying Future Leaders

A leader who fails to develop a successor fails. We must prayerfully identify future leaders and seek out those who display the following three characteristics:

Hunger

You can't develop someone who doesn't want to be developed. Look for hunger—people who are hungry for God, hungry to learn, and hungry for opportunity. We celebrate aspiration as described in 1 Timothy 3:1 (ESV): "The saying is trustworthy: If anyone aspires to the office of overseer, he desires a noble task."

There's a saying that "people can't hear you unless they are walking towards you." This is so important to recognize; otherwise, your development efforts will unnecessarily fall on bad soil. Not everyone is ready to be developed—not everyone is hungry. It's sad, but it's the truth. Spend your time developing those who are ready.

I've invested in many people over the years who were not hungry enough. I saw their gifts and potential, but the truth is, *I* wanted to see them grow and impact others more than *they* wanted to. Every time I have overlooked this, I have regretted it. Much of my effort has ended in frustration—a seemingly unfruitful investment. The opportunity cost of working hard to develop people who are not that hungry is that there are hungry people missing out. We have to acknowledge that sometimes, the people that show the most obvious promise are not hungry; meanwhile, the best people for the future are not the most obvious. Look beyond someone's gift because if there isn't hunger, the relationship is going to be one-sided. Development is a two-way street.

Humility

Humility is the key to all other virtues. Without it, nothing can be developed in the human soul—by God or by anyone else. As another saying goes, "When the student is ready, the teacher will appear." It's profound and true. A student's readiness has everything to do with humility. Humility is the ability to trust God and others with yourself. Humble people are teachable, and this is necessary if your development efforts are going to have a chance to be fruitful.

Honorable Character

Character trumps giftedness every day of the week, month, and year. Gifts take you places; character keeps you there. Look for people who have a developing character, living their lives in an increasingly honorable manner. Honorable character is formed when people live humble lives over time.

Jesus preached to the crowds, but He intentionally developed His disciples. In the same way, leaders love everybody, but they invest intentionally. Ask God for the ability to see people the way He does—to have the intuition regarding in whom to invest. Let the signs of hunger and humility be a guide to a process that should be led by God's Spirit. Invest in the people God brings your way.

Simultaneously develop more than one person as a future leader; it often doesn't take much more work to develop two or three people at the same time than it does one. In fact, developing people together can have the added benefits of camaraderie and peer development. Furthermore, if one of them doesn't work out (for Jesus, this was Judas), then you still have others that can continue on with the mission. If you want an investment to pay off, you don't put all your eggs in one basket. You diversify, and that's a great way to think about developing potential leaders.

The Process of Developing Future Leaders

Once you have identified two or three people who could be your next future leaders, have an intentional conversation to invite them into this development process. Use the principles from the chapter on recruitment, but remember to:

- Speak vision: tell them what you see they could become.

- Give clarity: explain the development process.
- Instill confidence: assure them that when they are ready, they will be commissioned.

> **Who people are is more important than what they do.**

The following is a helpful process for developing them to become leaders themselves. Each completed step should be followed by a debrief (see Appendix 4). Remember: each of these steps should be seen through the lens of being before doing because who people are is more important than what they do. The conversations and debriefs should focus on how our *being* impacts our *doing*. What is being developed in someone depends on how long this constant process may take. For a small group leader, it might take six months for this to be effective. Training someone for a simple service task may require only a month. For a more complex assignment (like prayer ministry), it may take a few more months. Developing a fantastic pastor might be a five-year process.

Watch Me!

Get them to explicitly observe you lead your group or team. Include them in all aspects, so they can see what happens in front of people *and* behind the scenes: preparation, follow-up, calls, and prayer. Take time to debrief with them, so they can ask questions about what they noticed. Your answers will help them understand not just what you do but why and how you do it.

Work With Me!

Include them in what you do as a leader. Allocate some of your leadership tasks to them. For example, have them run a specific part of a team meeting or be the one who sends out a communication email. Again, take time to debrief, so you can provide constructive and practical feedback to help them improve and grow in confidence. Discuss what you are both getting out of your being together.

I'll Watch You!

Let them become the interim leader with you watching. Let them handle the whole team for a week (or whatever period of time makes sense), or perhaps, put them in charge of a specific aspect of the team for a few weeks. Observe them, make notes, and give feedback. Encourage them and continue to give pointers to help them grow.

It's important to note that at this step, we are not expecting people to lead as well as us or exactly like us. We all have our own style! If they are 80 percent there, then that's more than good enough to move on to the next step. It's also important to reflect on how their being is affecting their doing.

You Do It!

Now we let them do it on their own without us around. We commission them and let them fly, but remember that your role in their development isn't over! Continue to check in with them, encourage them, and stay available for help and coaching when they need it. The ongoing support of a new leader is essential.

A Note About Transitioning a New Leader

We want to set up the group or team to receive their new leader well. Think about what needs to be communicated and to whom. Think about opportunities for feedback, questions, reservations, and conversations. Think about how much time is needed to adjust. Making yourself available to serve the transition is paramount.

A change in leadership is a leaving and cleaving time. People need time to celebrate what's been, grieve any loss that the change might bring, and adjust to the new person and what is to come. People often get lost, hurt, disillusioned, and disconnected during transitions. If we go a bit slower and become comfortable walking through a bit of mess as people process it, we will be stronger and more united on the other side.

Keep developing yourself, the people you lead, and future leaders.

To Lead is Good.
To Lead is to Be an Example.
To Lead is to Pray.
To Lead is to Grow in the Word.
To Lead is to Trust.
To Lead is to Learn.
To Lead is to Own It.
To Lead is to Care.
To Lead is to Serve.

To Lead is to Recruit.
To Lead is to Develop.

Put This Into Practice

1. On a scale of 1 to 5 (1 being the lowest and 5 being the highest), rate your team or group in the following areas:
   - Hunger: 1   2   3   4   5
   - Humility: 1   2   3   4   5
   - Honorable character: 1   2   3   4   5
2. What conversations and experiences can you have together to intentionally develop these people?
3. Pray and ask God which of those people you should plan to intentionally develop as leaders.

chapter 12
to lead is to build relationships

He aha te mea nui o te ao
He tangata, he tangata, he tangata

What is the most important thing in the world?
It is the people, it is the people, it is the people.
—Māori proverb

Every single person has a deep desire to be loved and to belong. These longings are only heightened in a world of what seems like ever-increasing relational brokenness. People have experienced family breakdown, absent parents, estrangement from wider family, and displacement from community due to work or political pressures. However, building relationships can often be overlooked. In a fast-paced world, which often wants to get straight down to business, we can't lose sight of our main jobs: loving God and loving people.

Most people we lead or will lead have major relational pain or trauma in their lives. A desire for community and the longing to have genuine friends often draw people towards churches and faith-based organizations.

This is where Jesus started. He recruited people into relationship with Him. His invitation to His would-be disciples was to first come to follow Him. But what did that following look like? It meant walking with Him, traveling with Him, waiting with Him, eating with Him, and helping Him minister to others. It meant building relationship with Him. Over the years, all of the great stuff the apostles would become and do would find its genesis in the relationship that was built. That's how it worked for Jesus; the disciples were with Him, over time, they became more like Him, and then they were able to do many of the things that He did.

> ## Our primary mandate is to build relationships with people.

Similarly, we need to recognize that our primary mandate is to build relationships with people. To get to know people, drink coffee with people, and have meals with people. We need to get into their lives and worlds and invite them into ours. Leadership doesn't have to be lonely if we remember to build real relationships. Building relationships is not a means to a greater end but needs to be seen by the leader as an end in itself. At the heart of leadership, if our desire is to help other people grow as disciples of Jesus, then we need to understand that it happens relationally. It's in the context of their relationship with us that we will be able to be an example to them.

Here are three thoughts that frame my view of building relationships as a leader:

1. Building relationships is like building a bridge.
   Our founding pastor always said, "You can't drive a ten-ton truck of truth over a one-ton bridge of friendship." As we get closer to people, we receive more permission to speak truthfully and lovingly into their lives. In his book The 5 Levels of Leadership, John Maxwell describes this as moving from positional leadership (people follow you because they have to; you have the title) to permission leadership (people follow you because they want to; there is relationship).[34]

2. Building relationships is enjoyable for the leader.
   Leading a small group, team, or project with people with whom you are also sharing daily life is satisfying. It's community; it's family. You realize there's something in it for you too. Leaders often forget that the church or faith-based organization in which they are leaders is for them too! God also wants to bless us, heal us, and make us whole through these relationships.

---

[34] John C. Maxwell, *The 5 Levels of Leadership: Proven Steps to Maximize Your Potential* (New York, NY: Center Street, 2011).

3. Building relationships is beautiful.
   Getting to know people, hearing their stories, and walking with them through the highs and lows of life are what make up the rich texture of living in a Jesus-centered community. It's Jesus-centered friendship because there's an extra party in the relationship. We find ourselves becoming the best of friends with the most unlikely people and come to see the multifaceted nature of God through the variety of people He brings into our lives.

Building Relationships Across a Whole Team or Group

We want to make time and make it a priority for the whole team or group to build relationships when we gather. Whether it's a group session or a team meeting, give time for people to simply chat. Sharing a meal at the table is powerful and opens people up. Give relationship-building the space it needs, and make time for people to pray for each other.

Create platforms for the group to be able to communicate with each other through group messaging or the like. Encourage people to ask for help, share their wins, and ask for prayer. All of this strengthens the relational ties across the group or team. Celebrate what's happening in people's lives (promotions, birthdays, anniversaries, etc.), and support people during times of need (sickness, moving house, having a new baby, etc.).

Building One-on-One Relationships

People are generally more vulnerable in a one-on-one setting compared to a larger group setting. Intentionally take time to get to know the people you lead on a deeper level. Make a plan to have each of your group or team members over individually for a meal a couple of times a year. If they have a spouse or family, invite them too. If that's not possible in your current season of life, go out for a coffee or a walk or meet their family at the local park. Encourage the people you lead to do this also!

Spending Extra Time With Two or Three

Jesus had twelve disciples, but within that twelve, there were three to whom He was closer than the others. If you read John's account of it, he considered himself the closest of the three (see John 20:2). I don't believe that Jesus simply clicked more with these three. Jesus intentionally and intensely invested in them. Two of those three went on to author part of the New Testament and featured prominently in the story of the early church.

We want to identify two to three people in our groups and on our teams that we can invest in at a deeper level. We, like Jesus, need to spend even more time with them. This strengthens our sense of having an inner circle, deepens our discipleship impact, and creates the opportunity for leadership development to happen. We will, one day, be able to replace ourselves or send out these close ones to become leaders themselves.

Research has shown that it's not whether people are in a group or a team that determines if they will grow in spiritual maturity—it's whether they are in spiritual community. It's possible to be in a group or a team and not function as a spiritual community. By committing ourselves, as leaders, to building relationships with Jesus as the center, we ensure that people will be planted in an environment that is conducive to their growth.

Relational Space

If you believe that you already have lots of friends and think you don't have any more space in your life for more people, then you're probably not ready to lead. We can't lead like Jesus if we don't have relational space in our lives. It doesn't mean ditching current relationships; it means transitioning and making space.

> **We can't lead like Jesus if we don't have relational space in our lives.**

A child matures as they grow up in the community of their home. Eventually, there comes a time for them to no longer live as intensely within those relational dynamics. They don't cut their parents or siblings off; they just create new space for additional relationships. When parents have more children, love multiplies—it doesn't divide. We can trust that God will guide us in this journey. As we create more relational space, He gives us more capacity.

Building relationships is very much the prize. Seeing people connected and in Jesus-centered community means that people have others to walk through the different seasons of life with. It means people have genuine friendships within their church. This is exactly what we are here for.

To Lead is Good.
To Lead is to Be an Example.
To Lead is to Pray.

To Lead is to Grow in the Word.
To Lead is to Trust.
To Lead is to Learn.
To Lead is to Own It.
To Lead is to Care.
To Lead is to Serve.
To Lead is to Recruit.
To Lead is to Develop.
To Lead is to Build Relationships.

Put This Into Practice

1. Do you have a plan for catching up—either one-on-one or in groups—with the people you lead?
2. Are you spending more time with the future leaders?
3. What could you do to develop a sense of family and fellowship with those you lead?

chapter 13

to lead is to have vision

"Vision without action is merely a dream. Action without vision just passes the time. Vision with action can change the world."
—Joel A. Barker[35]

Leaders need God-given, God-breathed, God-inspired vision. Eugene Peterson translates Proverbs 29:18 like this: "If people can't see what God is doing, they stumble all over themselves; But when they attend to what he reveals, they are most blessed" (MSG). We need to see what is possible and what God is calling us to do. Without vision, our groups and teams will stumble all over themselves.

---

35 Susan Ratcliffe, ed., *Oxford Essential Quotations 4th Edition* (New York, NY: Oxford University Press, 2016).

A vision is a desired picture of the future; it's the *why*. It's what we hope to achieve or become; it's why we are here and doing this thing! God gives vision. Every person in Scripture who found themselves face-to-face with God found themselves receiving a vision for their lives:

- Abraham heard God's voice calling him to a new place and to be a father of a nation.
- Moses heard God calling to him from the burning bush to be a rescuer of God's people.
- Gideon heard the Angel of the Lord calling him a mighty hero.
- Jeremiah heard God's voice through a vision calling him a prophet.
- Andrew and Peter heard Jesus's voice calling them to become fishers of men.
- The woman caught in adultery was given a vision from Jesus to sin no more.
- Paul received a vision to be an apostle rather than a persecutor.

When we encounter God, He gives us vision: vision for a life with Him, vision for a life to become like Him, and vision for being able to do the things He prepared for us since long ago (see Ephesians 2:10).

We Need a God-Vision

God's Word reveals to us a vision for our lives. This is most clearly seen in the Word that became flesh, the embodied Word—Jesus Christ. God's Word illuminates the path for every area of our lives, giving vision to guide our steps. His Word reveals who we are supposed to become, what we are supposed to be doing, and how we are supposed to be doing it. Scripture is obviously the main source of this revelation; however, we must also listen for the prophetic word that comes to specific situations in order to give vision.

> "Your word is a lamp to my feet and a light to my path."
> —Psalm 119:105 (ESV)

We need to make sure a vision is a God-vision, not just ambition. Over the years, I think we have come to realize that some of the great things we called "vision" were just ambition. These days, my team and I take a lot more time to discern God's words to us and involve others in testing the vision as we only ever want God's vision!

Nehemiah's story is helpful for clarifying a God-vision for the area entrusted to you. Nehemiah heard a report concerning his people who had returned to Jerusalem. He was told they were in trouble and shame, that the wall of Jerusalem had broken down and its gates destroyed by fire (see Nehemiah 1:3). This was a big deal in the ancient world. Without walls and gates, a city was defenseless, and its residents were vulnerable to constant raids and attacks.

The messenger's report moved Nehemiah's heart:

> As soon as I heard these words I sat down and wept and mourned for days, and I continued fasting and praying before the God of heaven.
> —Nehemiah 1:4 (ESV)

> **When seeking a vision, we need to get in touch with what moves our heart.**

When seeking a vision, we need to get in touch with what moves our heart. This is often the starting place of the discernment process—what has been left undone, what potential is not being realized, or what holy discontent is rising within us? What moves our heart can be the leading of God in our lives, calling us to be a part of the solution. It can be the genesis of a forming vision. It could be that young people don't know Jesus, that a people group in your church is not well cared for, or that more discipleship needs to take place. It could be to help someone in your life or to meet a need that's not currently being met. It's what moves your heart enough to feel something deeply and throws you into the presence of God in prayer. It's what moves our hearts enough that we would offer ourselves if God wills for us to be a part of leading a solution. This is the process Nehemiah went through:

- Nehemiah saw a problem and the opportunity within that problem.
- His heart was moved.
- He brought his heart into the presence of God through prayer and fasting.
- He offered himself as a servant to be a part of the solution.
- He emerged with a clear God-given vision to rebuild the wall of Jerusalem.

God has a vision for our lives and those under our influence and leadership. Let's make sure our vision is His vision and not just our ego's desire. Engaging in a process like Nehemiah's is a way to make sure that our vision is a God-vision; we will have God's grace over the fulfillment of the vision if it is!

We Need a Vision Worth Sacrificing For

Before I became the lead pastor of Curate Church, I led our community missions area. I sensed God was giving me a vision to lead our church to rebuild someone's house in our local community—*Extreme Makeover* style, if you have ever heard of that show! The crew would turn up as a surprise to some well-deserving person's home, send them away on a holiday, then hustle like crazy all week to completely renovate and improve their home before the big reveal when they returned home. Inspired by the show (and the Holy Spirit), I received permission from my pastor to pursue the idea.

I reached out to a community organization, and we partnered with them to choose the right family and home. We took a camera crew around to their place to let them know that in a few months' time, we were going to send them away and give their home an extreme makeover in preparation for a family reunion. They were blown away and incredibly grateful. I was overwhelmed. I wished that I had seen the home before I committed to the project. It was falling apart. It was almost unsuitable for occupants. I even fell through a rotten part of the floor while touring the house. We were literally in over our heads!

But we had come too far to turn back; the only way was forwards. I assembled a team, raised the money to pay for it all, and arranged sponsorships for materials and construction crews—all while continually telling the story of the family and casting a vision for their reunion. It was 2009—the global recession was afoot, but that didn't stop people from giving their products, time, and money to see the vision turn into a reality. Within three months, we had all the money and materials needed, and the family was sent away on a holiday to pick up their grandparents from overseas. Over the course of ten days, we made the impossible possible with hundreds of volunteers working around the clock.

Seeing this family reunited in a healthy home was a vision worth sacrificing for. As people responded to and rallied around this vision, it caused people to rise to a new level in service and generosity. It brought out the "gold" in people I would have never expected to get involved. It revealed that people were capable of much more than I had thought. You will be amazed at how people rise to the occasion when there's a vision worth sacrificing for. It's sometimes tempting for leaders to have a small vision—or no vision—because they don't want to put people out or ask too much of them. In doing so, they rob them of the joy of sacrifice and the satisfaction of achieving something demanding.

A Vision Keeps Us Focused

I'm a novice chess player at best. I love playing with my kids, and they often beat me. But this principle can be seen in the game of chess: there is a clear vision that keeps you focused. In chess, that vision is to get your opponent into a checkmate situation—and if you can't do that, at least end up in a stalemate! The goal isn't to take more pieces than the other or to get your pieces to the other side. Because that goal, vision, or end result is clear, it helps you make specific decisions. You sacrifice pawns for greater pieces, you give up pieces for positions on the board, and you hope that by living in line with your vision, you will win.

> **If everything's important, then nothing's important.**

In the same way, a vision within our church and faith-based organizational contexts keeps us focused and calls us upwards. A vision claims there's something that isn't yet a reality that is more important than something that is. If everything's important, then nothing's important. When we have a vision worth sacrificing for, it helps those we lead and us to prioritize, sacrifice, and make strategic decisions. There were many times during the home makeover project journey in which choices had to be made regarding the budget, design, timelines, and products. Having a clear vision for a reunited family and a healthy home gave us a filter through which to run these decisions. It kept us focused and on track.

Observations of a God-Vision in Action

As this chapter draws to a close, I want to share three main observations of a God-vision in action. Consider them indicators of a healthy vision.

It Supports a "Bigger" Vision

Your church, pastor, leader, or organization has a vision for the area you lead. Your vision needs to support the bigger vision.

Curate Church's vision is "to be a people pursuing the way of Jesus and playing our part in His story." This vision outworks itself through the kids' program to the youth group and the small groups to the community missions. But it's important that every leader's and every area's vision support this main vision. More than one vision creates division. When we have a vision that's contributing to the overall vision, that's unity. And unity attracts the Lord's blessing:

> How good and pleasant it is
>   when God's people live together in unity!
> It is like precious oil poured on the head,
> running down on the beard,
> running down on Aaron's beard,
> down on the collar of his robe.
> It is as if the dew of Hermon
> were falling on Mount Zion.
> For there the Lord bestows his blessing,
> even life forevermore. —**Psalm 133 (NIV)**

Before I shift to my second observation, I want to briefly share some thoughts in relation to leading someone else's vision. It requires maturity and integrity. It's often not a lack of vision that's the problem but the inability to get everyone to support it. If you're leading a team in an area that's part of a larger vision, I want to encourage you to be an amplifier, not a parrot. Let me explain.

Parrots can repeat words people say, but they don't have comprehension. A leader can say all the right words, but it's not convincing because the words are internalized. They don't believe what they are saying. They haven't bought into it. Amplifiers work differently. They take the input, sound, or message, internalize and process it, and then, express it as output with an even louder volume. Let's be like that! We want to receive the vision, process it, wrestle with it, support it, and add our weight and voice to it, so it resounds even louder.

It Aims for the Possible—Not Just the Passable

Imagine if your vision for your team wasn't just to get the job done but to see the area improve and the people on your team flourish. A God-vision is not about what we can get away with or the minimum with which we can scrape by. It's about what could be—what is *possible* with God's help, not just passable through our own efforts. Vision should raise the bar and include a "God-gap"—a space in which we need God to turn up if it's going to be fulfilled. Having a vision to start a discipleship group that meets for a couple of hours each week is one thing. That same vision with a "God-gap" includes the desire to see that weekly gathering turn into a genuine community of people who share the ups and downs of life on a daily basis. A leader can make the first version of this vision a reality. The Holy Spirit is needed to make the second version happen.

It Is Spoken About Often

A God-vision gets people excited, and as a result, they speak about it often. Keep the wording simple, repeatable, and memorable. When we have a clear vision that people know and speak about often, we're well on our way to having more people rally around that vision. Vision can leak, and mission can drift, so speak it often. Tell stories that illustrate it. An easy way to think about it is to continue talking about the *why* and not just the *what*. Every time your team gathers, remind them of why they do what they do; tell them stories that highlight the why and how it's having an impact and making a difference.

A vision is like a fire—it will fizzle out if you leave it for a while without putting more wood on it. Keep the vision's fire burning hot by constantly throwing on more wood of language, story, and celebration!

To Lead is Good.
To Lead is to Be an Example.
To Lead is to Pray.
To Lead is to Grow in the Word.
To Lead is to Trust.
To Lead is to Learn.
To Lead is to Own It.
To Lead is to Care.
To Lead is to Serve.
To Lead is to Recruit.
To Lead is to Develop.
To Lead is to Build Relationships.
To Lead is to Have Vision.

Put This Into Practice

Reflect and journal on the following questions:
1. What is your church's or organization's vision?
2. What area do you lead, and which people does that area involve?
3. Is there already a vision for the area you lead? What is it?
4. How can your area contribute to the bigger vision?
5. What could be possible in your area with the Holy Spirit's power?
6. What is it about your area that moves your heart, gets you up in the morning, and causes you to pray?
7. How can you express the vision in a way that is simple, repeatable, and memorable?

chapter 14

to lead is to shape culture

"Culture is built through the stories we tell and the heroes we make."
—Erwin McManus

Culture is "how things are done around here." It is created by design or default and can be healthy or unhealthy, God-honoring, or Spirit-grieving. Culture is shaped by our vision (our why), our values (our behaviors), our leaders (our heroes and examples), our stories, and our communication. In the previous chapter, I unpacked the power of vision, which is the starting point when it comes to shaping culture. Having a compelling and inspiring why and unifying people around it is the primary task of a leader. This chapter focuses on three aspects of culture-shaping.

Aspect 1: Defining Values

Shaping culture begins to take place by defining what we value. What we value can be seen in the way we act, what we celebrate, and what we confront. Imagine embarking on an ancient sea voyage. You're the captain. You have recruited a crew, prepared all the supplies, and made the vision clear. In this case, it's the destination—perhaps unknown lands beyond the horizon. With that in everyone's minds, you set sail.

At some point, a storm hits. You lose some supplies, the crew gets stressed, and they start to turn on each other. You try to regain control, but now they turn on you. Your first mate sides with the crew rather than you—their captain. You have a full-blown mutiny on your hands. This has happened throughout history on countless occasions, derailing journeys on the precipice of discovery, costing people's lives, and leaving many great visions unfulfilled.

This is not a vision problem. It's a values problem.

A church's or faith-based organization's culture is its collective way of operating. It determines what is acceptable and unacceptable. It comes with its own tone, way of speaking, and way of relating. It creates distinctive strengths and weaknesses. No group can endure for any substantial period of time without developing some patterns of leadership, differentiation of roles among its members, means of managing conflict, ways of articulating shared values and norms, and some supervision to assure acceptable levels of conformity to those norms.

There are two types of cultures—both with interconnected values—that leaders need to cultivate: kingdom culture and organizational culture. The following values unpack this. This is not an exhaustive list but ones that I have found to be core to my own leadership experience.

Kingdom Culture and Related Values

Kingdom culture is the most important type of culture to shape within your church or faith-based organization. It's more important than building your brand. Biblical values are more important than organizational values. Any kingdom-centered organization should only be giving voice and language ultimately to values of the kingdom of God. Kingdom culture keeps us aligned with Jesus and what He wants to bring forth in us, through us, and around us.

Love

Kingdom culture is a culture first marked by love. It's like the Pete Scazzero quote from chapter 8: "Make love be the measure of maturity."[36] Love *is* the measure of maturity in the kingdom of God. Not just any type of love though—*agape* love—a self-giving love that wills the good of another as modeled by Jesus through His crucifixion.

Truth

Jesus was full of grace and truth (see John 1:14). True worshipers worship the Father in Spirit and truth (see John 4:23), and truth is required to love. If to love is to will the good of another, there needs to be a definition of what that "good" is. This is where truth comes in. Truth provides God's definition of what is good

---

36 Peter Scazzero, *Emotionally Healthy Discipleship: Moving from Shallow Christianity to Deep Transformation.*

so that we are able to be a Spirit-empowered presence in the lives of others, leading them towards it. "Love does not delight in evil but rejoices with the truth" (1 Corinthians 13:6, NIV).

The Fruit of the Spirit

Galatians 5:22-23 lists the fruit of the Spirit. The first three of the nine listed are the most important—love, joy, and peace. The other six are the by-products. These were the markers of Jesus's life on earth. Therefore, we need to partner with the Spirit to shape cultures of love, joy, and peace.

> ## You can't create a culture around you that first isn't in you.

Back in chapter 2, I explored the need for a leader to be an example. This also applies here; you can't create a culture around you that first isn't in you. We need to be people who can sit across from each other in the aisles of disagreement and still exhibit the fruit of the Spirit. We need to be people who model and are growing in love, joy, and peace. We need to be leaders who are encouraging others to become love, joy, and peace. We need to relate to each other through the lenses of love, joy, and peace. Paul wrote to the church in Colossi, "Let the peace of Christ rule in your hearts, since as members of one body you were called to peace. And be thankful" (Colossians 3:15, NIV). What does it look like for peace to rule in our lives and churches?

Holiness

First Peter 1:16 (NIV) reminds us of what Scripture says regarding holiness: "Be holy, because I am holy." Of course, all of us fall short of God's holiness—that's what the forgiveness offered through Christ's blood is for. But His mercy also comes with grace, and that grace is God's empowerment to live a life pleasing to the Father—set apart, holy, and pure.

Much is written in the New Testament about taking off the old person and putting on the new, running from old ways of living and seeking new ways. Kingdom culture takes the pursuit of such a life seriously. We pursue this according to Jesus's teaching in the Sermon on the Mount by becoming the type of person who wants to and naturally lives this way out of a transformed inner world.

Organization Culture and an Example of Values

The church or faith-based organization of which you are a part no doubt has its own cultural quirks and style. It will have its own common language. We need to be people who are growing in our understanding of the culture of the organization in which we play a part. We need to be learning to be people who cascade the culture—as it flows to us, we need to be conduits of it, enabling the culture to flow to those we lead.

This has never been more important than it is right now. We are all a part of both in-person and digital communities. Both of these are trying to form us. People often give more weight and shaping influence to the online networks to which they are connected than the embodied community in which God has placed them. If we are going to be effective leaders in our communities, we need to be aware of the voices shaping us and the messages we are receiving and passing on.

During the COVID-19 pandemic, it became clear to me, as a pastor, that although some people attended the church I pastored, I wasn't actually considered *their* pastor. They were not leaning into what we sensed God was saying to us as we journeyed through the pandemic as a community. Instead, they listened to their networks, YouTube algorithms, Facebook groups, and podcasts. To be clear, I'm not writing about people's different stances on lockdowns, vaccines, and other restrictions. I'm referring to people's different stances on living faithfully for Christ during that time.

Our church, generally speaking, was comprised of two distinct groups of people that ended up in very different places over the course of two years (2020 and 2021). There were those who leaned in, listened, and tried to journey with their community. Their relationships grew closer, stronger, deeper, and more peaceful. Then, there were those who did the opposite. They became disconnected, divisive, anxious, and pained.

Leaders need to be mindful of the influence that networks outside of embodied organizations have on those we lead and help people intentionally lean into their embodied communities. Those who have invited you to lead are trusting that you will lead people in the direction in which the community or organization is traveling as a whole. We want to shape cultures of unity—not mutiny!

We want to shape cultures of unity—not mutiny!

The church that I lead has five core values. While we want to value everything that Scripture teaches us to value, our core values are the things we want to emphasize in any given season if we are to continue to travel towards our vision in a kingdom-aligned manner. Our core values also address things that don't necessarily come naturally within our unique, wider cultural context.

Here are our five core values:

1. Love—Aroha

    We love because God first loved us. His love is what the Bible refers to as agape—the unconditional and highest form of love—which I wrote about previously. We want to be people with this type of love, who do everything out of agape because without this love, it all counts for nothing. We love our Heavenly Father, we love our Lord and Savior, Jesus Christ, and we love His Holy Spirit with all our heart, soul, mind, and strength. We love others the way we love ourselves.

2. Gospel and Mission—Rongopai

    We believe that God is making all things new through the power of His kingdom. We are called and committed to a life of mission—here and now. Playing our part in God's redemptive story, we offer up our whole lives and vocations as a crucial part of the outworking of His mission. We want everyone to have a chance to hear the good news of Jesus and

His kingdom in a way they can understand, from someone they can trust, and with a power that's transformational.

3. Spiritual Practices—Tikanga Wairua

    We are committed to growing in spiritual practices, both communally and individually. Spiritual practices are our way of making ourselves available and open to God's grace—the Spirit of God working in us in order to transform us. Such practices are ways of setting our minds upon things above. Spiritual practices are ways of intentionally learning to be with Jesus, becoming like Jesus, and doing the things Jesus would do if He were us in this world.

4. Togetherness—Whanaungatanga

    We describe ourselves as family and whānau because church is more than a community. The common metaphor used to describe the people of God in the New Testament is that of brothers and sisters. God is forming us into a loving family. We believe that we learn how to follow Jesus more fully in the context of this family of faith and grace. We thrive when we celebrate God's goodness together and learn how to be like Jesus through the sharing of our journeys.

5. Authenticity—Tūturutanga

    We bring our true and whole selves to the whānau . Our Heavenly Father accepts us on the basis of His mercy and grace made available to us through the sacrifice of His Son, Jesus—not on the basis of our performance. Therefore, we are free to live honestly before God and others. Living a life of openness and vulnerability reminds us that we are all on a journey. We are a community that talks about things as they really are and does our best to "keep it real." We aspire to truly live out what we talk about.

We desire that the leaders within our specific church foster a culture that lives out these values in their groups, teams, and ministries. For example, every time that our teams gather, we encourage them to talk about, tell stories, and illustrate how they can practice and apply one of the core values.

As I conclude this aspect of defining values, I want you to think about shaping culture through the eyes of a gardener and farmer. God is a wonderful teacher, and He gives the farmer great wisdom (see Isaiah 28:29). Paul also wrote that he *planted seeds* in hearts and that Apollos *watered* them, but it was God who made them *grow* (see 1 Corinthians 3:6). We are cultivating culture. It's not an exact science or a closed-loop linear system. It has variables and requires the wisdom and tenderness of a master gardener who continually reflects on these questions:

- What needs to be planted?
- What needs to be watered?
- What needs to be weeded?

Aspect 2: Building Values

Once values are defined, we need to lead the process of building them! The following three Ls have immensely helped me—and the leaders on my team—to do this.

Lines

This L is about what we accept and what we don't and what we tolerate and what we don't. Some of these are explicit; others are unspoken. There was a motivational poster in my high school mathematics class that said, "If you stand for nothing, you'll fall for anything."

Our national rugby team, the famous All Blacks, has an expectation that the person who wins Player of the Match is also the person who cleans up the locker room at the end of the match. This is a line they have drawn to shape a humble culture. What will your lines be?

Lines are essentially expectations regarding important areas like engagement, attendance, accountability, communication, and timelines. When people step over those lines, we need to work out how to respond. You don't need lots of rules, but you do need to draw some lines. Shaping a healthy culture will require clarity about how the church or faith-based organization is committed to working together and growing together. Think about the lines, discuss the lines, and articulate the lines. Keep it simple and hold each other accountable.

Leaders

This L is about the stories we tell and the heroes we make. The heroes of our culture are those who are promoted to leadership. So, if you have been invited to lead, you need to be an example of the desired culture and hold yourself to a higher standard than someone who has not. You must first be whatever it is you want to see in others. As you identify future leaders you want to develop and deploy, think about whether they will make the culture better or worse. If we have a thousand "Johns," would we have a thousand blessings or a thousand problems? People in both formal leadership positions and perceived leadership positions (such as being on the platform or having public opportunities to give opinions) shape the culture, whether we realize it or not and whether it's beneficial or not.

Language

This L is about how our culture is identified, defined, and transmitted through words. Every culture around the world is identifiable by its unique language. The same applies to our churches and faith-based organizations. We need to teach those in our groups and on our teams to be mindful of what our church or organization is talking about in a particular season and to ensure they are doing what they can to pass the message on. The apostle Paul encouraged Timothy to pass on his teachings and messages to trustworthy people who were capable of passing them on to others (see 2 Timothy 2:2).

Aspect 3: Communicating and Celebrating Values

We shape culture every time we communicate. From phone calls to text messages and from social media posts to emails—all of it shapes culture. How we communicate, how we talk about people and topics, and what we choose to say and not say all shape culture.

As leaders, we need to be intentional about how we communicate with people during face-to-face interactions and over other media. These are always opportunities to reinforce and promote the desired culture. We strengthen the desired culture when we can connect our topics of conversation back to the vision and core values. We also shape and strengthen culture when we tell stories about and celebrate people and milestones that are connected to the vision and core values.

> **Patterns of celebration, along with the weekly practice of Sabbath, were designed to help people learn to live well in God's good creation.**

I love that God commanded the people of Israel to celebrate! They gathered at least three times a year for festivals of celebration, remembrance, and worship. These patterns of celebration, along with the weekly practice of Sabbath, were designed to help people learn to live well in God's good creation. These practices have the ability to hold people to what's important and keep people from drifting. Much like the annual celebrations of Christmas and Thanksgiving pull us back to our families and loved ones, intentionally celebrating with those we lead energizes our groups and teams. We need to remind each other of how far we have come and that we are making a difference. Celebration gives us the opportunity to reflect, share, and bring to mind what God is doing within us and through us. It gives people a sense of how their efforts are contributing to the difference being made by the whole community.

We can celebrate the people we lead—the important occasions and milestones in their lives. We can celebrate the progress we are making. We can celebrate when someone exhibits behavior that reflects our values. We can celebrate stories of life change. We can celebrate a job well done. We can celebrate how our team or group contributed to an organizational or church-wide effort. We can celebrate the start or end of a season.

During our weekly staff meetings, we take time to celebrate different people on our team. We celebrate things we have seen others do that we like and appreciate. We have cards that people can fill in to "brag about" their chosen person. This intentional time of celebration energizes people, shapes culture, and builds greater bonds between us. Celebration can take on lots of different forms; just make sure it's part of the rhythm within your church or faith-based organization.

To Lead is Good.
To Lead is to Be an Example.
To Lead is to Pray.
To Lead is to Grow in the Word.
To Lead is to Trust.
To Lead is to Learn.
To Lead is to Own It.
To Lead is to Care.
To Lead is to Serve.
To Lead is to Recruit.
To Lead is to Develop.
To Lead is to Build Relationships.
To Lead is to Have Vision.
To Lead is to Shape Culture.

Put This Into Practice

1. What is your plan for helping the people you lead lean into the culture of your church or organization?
2. How often do you pray with your team for the whole church or organization?
3. Plan to share a story or a devotion about one of your values and connect it with your work each time you get together.
4. What stories need to be told?
5. What heroes need to be celebrated?
6. What attitudes or behaviors need to be graciously confronted?
7. Pray the "Prayer for Peace" frequently attributed to Saint Francis of Assisi:

    Lord, make me an instrument of your peace:
    where there is hatred, let me sow love;
    where there is injury, pardon;
    where there is doubt, faith;
    where there is despair, hope;
    where there is darkness, light;
    where there is sadness, joy.

    O divine Master, grant that I may not so much seek
    to be consoled as to console,
    to be understood as to understand,
    to be loved as to love.
    For it is in giving that we receive,
    it is in pardoning that we are pardoned,
    and it is in dying that we are born to eternal life.
    Amen.

conclusion

embark on the voyage

> *"Even youths will become weak and tired, and young men will fall in exhaustion. But those who trust in the Lord will find new strength. They will soar high on wings like eagles. They will run and not grow weary. They will walk and not faint."*
> —Isaiah 40:30-31 (NLT)

If I were to have written this book four years ago, in my naivety, I wouldn't have included this chapter—but now I know better. I've been there—I've come face-to-face with the depths of burnout. After years in ministry, incredible growth, an amazing team, and lots of fun (and our fair share of problems and failure), I hit the wall. I woke up one day, and for the first time ever didn't want to be a pastor anymore. I was spent physically, drained of my energy. I was spent spiritually; my soul didn't want to pray. I was spent relationally and found myself withdrawing from everyone.

I was done. With the exhaustion, depression, and anxiety that quickly followed, I was looking everywhere for a way out.

I'm super thankful for my wife, Katie, my kids, and my board and staff who were patient with me, carried the load, and found a way for us to all continue on while I recovered. Now, nearly three years on, I'm almost back to full capacity. My energy has returned to a new normal, my spirit is more alive than ever, my relationships are richer, the depression has passed, and I'm excited, once again, for what I get to do and whom I get to do it with. In fact, I'm just about to return after a holiday, and I've been excited to get back for several days now.

There's a huge propensity for burnout when you work with people and are in leadership. From compassion and empathy fatigue to carrying the weight of responsibility, it's so easy to be worn down over time. Add to that the complexities of modern life, and it's no wonder we see so many people burning out.

As a leader, there is a possibility of it happening to you too. As you become a good leader—maybe even a great one—you will be highly involved in people's lives while carrying responsibility. The challenge will become how to lead sustainably over not just the seasons but the years and decades so that by God's grace, you can have an ever-multiplying impact on people.

As you get better at leading, you may find yourself being promoted. You will find you will be asked to take on more. If you have led a great group, you might be asked to oversee other group leaders. If you have brought great health and life to one department or ministry, you may be asked to take on another. These opportunities may be from God, and I hope they come your way.

Inevitably though, eventually, opportunities will come your way that you will need to learn to say no to.

I think God would rather have us lead faithfully and well over the course of our lives than take on too much and only be able to lead for a short season. We may need to say no to our pastor, our leader, or our boss. We may need to learn to say no to some of our extracurricular activities. We may need to say no to some opportunities at work, so we can keep leading in our church faithfully.

Seasons come and go, and demands change as our life moves onwards. I want to give you a metaphor that I have found incredibly helpful for learning to roll with the changes while trying to be faithful and consistent with the people I lead. It's that of a dimmer switch. Sometimes people like to use the on and off switch when it comes to involvement and leadership—some seasons, they are on, and others, they are off. There are certainly times when that's called for.

> **I liken role in leadership to a dimmer switch. I roll with the seasons and adjust the intensity of my involvement to suit.**

I, however, like the dimmer switch: rolling with the seasons and adjusting the intensity of my involvement to suit. When the kids are sick, I might have to turn the switch down a bit to provide care and be present with them. When everyone's doing well, and home is taken care of, I have more to give and greater availability to offer to the people I lead. There are times in the year I find it easy to preach week in and week out and others when that wouldn't be wise. All of this is to say, as a leader, learn to say a good, yet godly, no at the right times for the sake of longevity.

I remember singing a worship song to the Lord very passionately on a Sunday morning many years ago. It was the song *Oceans*. It uses the story of Jesus and Peter walking on water to encourage faith and bold followership of Jesus. I remember re-laying my life down to Him, saying, "I'll go wherever you send me. I'll do whatever you want." I was a lead pastor already, but I didn't want to settle. I didn't want to become too comfortable, so I put it all on the line again.

So, there I was, ready to sell up and move across the world to start some new initiative or just do anything that God asked me to do. I was singing, I was on my knees, and I was stirred and full of faith. I was waiting for the Lord to speak. And He did speak: *I love you, and I'm proud of you, son.*

That's it. Initially, I was a bit disappointed. But the words had a potency that deeply impacted me. I sat with them, and they began to minister to the depths of my soul. I wanted to do great things for God, but God wanted to have a moment of intimacy with me.

This leadership journey is wild. It's embarking on the great unknown. It's pushing out into the ever-changing seascape. It involves the waves of pressure, the winds of distraction, and the storms of other people's lives. It's also got the peace and stillness of a glassy ocean, the beauty and joy of dancing dolphins, and the depths of the deep blue sea.

Signing up to lead will mean sometimes staying when you want to go and going when you want to stay. There's nothing like leadership to grow you, stretch you, and press you. But there's something about that pressing that releases an oil—an oil that illuminates, provides, and heals. As we give away our lives in and for Jesus, we find our lives. We get to see people's lives eternally changed, their freedom renews ours, their breakthrough becomes our joy, and their restoration, growth, and wholeness permeate our life in the best of ways.

> **As we give away our lives in and for Jesus, we find our lives.**

We get a front-row seat to God's grace. We see Him move, heal, provide, restore, save, and transform even the hardest of hearts. My journey of leadership has cost me so much, but it's given me more than I could ever give.

Embrace the call of God on your life to lead, lean into His strength and wisdom to do it in love, persevere, endure, stay in the game, and over the years, you will see God multiply your impact and do something in you and around you that you could only have dreamed about.

To lead, after all, is an adventure, and the boarding ticket is a simple yes.

notes

appendix 1:
spiritual practices

The Spirit of the Disciplines: Understanding How God Changes Lives by Dallas Willard
Celebration of Discipline by Richard J. Foster
https://www.practicingtheway.org
Spiritual Disciplines Handbook: Practices That Transform Us by Adele Ahlberg Calhoun

appendix 2:
theology resources

Theosu.ca
Baker Encyclopedia of the Bible
Systematic Theology by Wayne Grudem

appendix 3:
meeting template

People to Recruit:	Meeting Booked For:	Had the Meeting:	Follow Up On:	Outcome:

TO LEAD

People to Recruit:	Meeting Booked For:	Had the Meeting:	Follow Up On:	Outcome:

appendix 4:
debrief template

Step one — Watch me
1. What did you notice?
2. Why do you think I went about it that way?
3. Who do you need to become to do things this way as a natural expression of who you are?

Step two — Work with me
1. What went well?
2. What are one or two areas in need of further growth or consideration?
3. How did our formation and preparation inform our actions?

Step three — I'll watch you
1. What did you learn?

2. What did you do well?
3. What will you work on in the future?

Step four—You do it
1. How do you think you are going?
2. In what ways do you need support?
3. How can I continue to encourage you going forward?

On going support questions:
1. How are your rhythms and time with Jesus?
2. How is your marriage or singleness going?
3. Tell me about your top 1-3 priorities/goals and the challenges you are facing?
4. What is your next step for development and growth—both personally and in your ministry.

about the author

Joel Milgate is the lead pastor of Curate Church, a multi-location church in New Zealand. He has been in ministry for seventeen years. Curate has experienced incredible growth under his leadership. Together with his wife, Katie, they bring a vision for what the church could be, authenticity, and family values. Joel is a mentor to pastors, passionate about church planting, and motivated by the desire to see people pursue the way of Jesus and play their part in His story. Joel and Katie live in Tauranga, New Zealand, with their four children: Alessandro, Micah, Charlie, and Violet.

AVAIL +

TRY FOR 30 DAYS *AND RECEIVE*
THE SEQUENCE TO SUCCESS
BUNDLE *FREE*

$79 VALUE

+ BOOK
+ STUDY GUIDE
+ ONLINE COURSE
+ LIVE CLASS
+ MORE

The Art *of* Leadership

This isn't just another leadership collective...this is the next level of networking, resources, and empowerment designed specifically for leaders like you.

Whether you're an innovator in ministry, business, or your community, **AVAIL +** is designed to take you to your next level. Each one of us needs connection. Each one of us needs practical advice. Each one of us needs inspiration. **AVAIL +** is all about equipping you, so that you can turn around and equip those you lead.

THEARTOFLEADERSHIP.COM/CHAND

THE AVAIL PODCAST

HOSTED BY VIRGIL SIERRA

CLAIM YOUR *FREE* ANNUAL SUBSCRIPTION

FreeAvailOffer.com

To claim your subscription ($59 value)

SCAN HERE TO LEARN MORE

YOU HAVE A MESSAGE THAT NEEDS TO BE HEARD

IT'S TIME TO INNOVATE THE WAY WE PACKAGE OUR MESSAGE AND BRING IT TO MARKET!

"If I had Martijn in my life in my earlier years, my messaging and impact could have been much greater. However, better late than never. Martijn has revolutionized my life. I trust him explicitly. He is in charge of all I do, from concept to completion. He has made my world larger and he can do the same for you."
—Sam Chand

TO CLAIM A FREE COPY OF UNLEASHED
THEARTOFLEADERSHIP.COM/UNLEASHED

www.ingramcontent.com/pod-product-compliance
Lightning Source LLC
Chambersburg PA
CBHW070532090426
42735CB00013B/2962

WHAT PEOPLE ARE SAYING ABOUT **TO LEAD**

"A long-time friend of Maree's and mine, Pastor Joel has an amazing leadership gift and desire to build kingdom culture. His fresh take on leadership encourages us that leading is something we are all called to do and that God is looking for leaders and volunteers just like you and me. With Jesus as our ultimate example, the leading of the Holy Spirit, and practical wisdom, we can bring what we have and watch what God can do with it. With insightful examples and helpful tools to *put this into practice* at the end of each chapter, this book will truly make a difference to leaders at all levels."

—Pastor Paul de Jong
Founding Pastor, LIFE New Zealand and Australia, and author of *God Money & Me*

"Joel pastors a strong, vibrant church and is a thoughtful, engaging leader. His voice is critical, and this book will broaden and deepen your love for God and the church."

—Nathan Finochio
Founder of TheosU and TheosSeminary, Teaching Pastor, and Author of *Hearing God* and *Killer Church*

"This book is an excellent guide for aspiring leaders within the church. We have known Joel and Katie for many years and have watched them apply the principles that he has presented in this book. The results have been truly fruitful. They have produced leaders within the church that are more than capable and lead by example in their service. I can say that Joel has and is living the principles that he has laid out, and many have benefited from the information that he has imparted. If you have people looking to become part of a leadership team, this provides great guidelines to follow to develop men and women in the service of God."

—Tom Brock
Wave of Life Ministries International

"This book will take your leadership to new levels. Joel addresses many of the questions and apprehensions that all leaders face, giving the reader insight and a strategy to develop their leadership skills. This book will encourage and equip you to be the leader God created you to be."

—Dr. J. Todd Mullins
Christ Fellowship Church

"I have had the joy of knowing Joel Milgate (and Katie and the kids) for many years. I have watched him at home, in his office, at the weekend services of Curate, and among his contemporaries. Joel is a curious leader who is constantly rethinking the normal ways of doing things. Being a local church pastor, his practical skills afford him the opportunity to write on leadership for those currently serving as well as those aspiring to do so. May this serve you as a way to navigate your leadership journey in a way that betters serves all those around you."

—Joel A'Bell
Oceania Regional Leader, Convoy of Hope